155.937 Harvey, Carol
D. H.

The Sunshine
widows

1895

The Sunshine
Widows

The Sunshine Widows

Adapting to Sudden Bereavement

Carol D.H. Harvey
Boise State University
Howard M. Bahr
Brigham Young University

LexingtonBooks
D.C. Heath and Company
Lexington, Massachusetts
Toronto

Library of Congress Cataloging in Publication Data

Harvey, Carol D H
    The Sunshine widows.

    1. Sunshine Mine Disaster, Kellogg, Idaho, 1972. 2. Widows—Idaho—
Psychology. 3. Mine accidents—Idaho—Psychological aspects.
I. Bahr, Howard M., joint author. II. Title.
TN315.H35   155.9'37   79-8317
ISBN 0-669-03375-8

Published simultaneously in Canada.

Printed in the United States of America.

International Standard Book Number: 0-669-03375-8

Library of Congress Catalog Card Number: 79-8317

*For Ruth and Ida, widows for a time,
and inspirational to the authors.*

Contents

List of Figures

List of Tables

Acknowledgments

The authors would like to thank the subjects—widows and other women of the Coeur d'Alene mining district—who talked to us at length in 1972, and some of whom talked again in 1977. They gave freely of their time and energy, telling their stories, which were sometimes painful and always interesting, in order that we could share their ideas and impressions. Without their cooperation, the book could not have been written.

To the granting agencies, the National Institute of Mental Health for the 1972 study (# 1 RD 3 MH 23496-01) and the State of Idaho for the 1977 restudy, we also give our thanks. Encouragement and guidance was provided particularly by Stephanie B. Stolz, Small Grants Section Chief of NIMH in 1972. Richard Hart, of the Boise State University Bureau of Research, Grants, and Contracts, was also very helpful.

Our interest in the topic of widowhood stems in part from the influence of Felix Berardo. The use of comparison samples to provide a context within which the widows' experiences could be judged was recommended by A. Robert Corbin of Boise State University. Guidance, inspiration, and patience were also provided by our spouses, Mahlon O. Harvey and Rosemary F. Smith Bahr.

The two field directors for the research, Evelyn Montague and Sylvia Watts, also deserve thanks. We are indebted to the many interviewers we hired in the Coeur d'Alene River Valley, and particularly to Laura Williamson and Ginny Seymour, who worked after the survey in 1972 to help widows raise money and erect a monument to the dead men, and to Carol Stacey, who publicized our research.

Editorial assistance was provided by Kay Grant Powers, who had been an interviewer in 1972, and by Ruth E. Hussa, herself a widow and mother to the senior author. Work-study assistance was provided by undergraduate research assistants Sharon Royston and Jacqueline Drake at Boise State University. JoAnna McKay Rhoades, of Brigham Young University, patiently typed and retyped the manuscript. Assistance in computer analysis was given under the direction of Harvey Capell and Emerson C. Maxson at Boise State University and by Rod Jackson at Brigham Young University.

Carl Griner, Idaho State Inspector of Mines, and his assistant William Bondurant as well as James P. Farris, Personnel Director of the Sunshine Mining Company, lent their essential cooperation. H.F. Magnuson, who oversees the spending of the Miners' Memorial Educational Fund, also cooperated in the research. Also involved are the sociologists who inspired us along the way and the friends who provided personal inspiration. In the latter category is Ida Harvey Coe, herself a widow for twenty-two years.

To all of these people and to the unnamed others whose assistance made this research possible, we express appreciation.

The Sunshine
Widows

1 The Fire

The Coeur d'Alene River winds through northern Idaho about a hundred miles south of the Canadian border. The old Mullan Road, built to supplement the Oregon Trail as a road to the Northwest, crossed the river a score of times in northern Idaho and opened the area to settlers and prospectors. In fact, the Mullan Road across northern Idaho was barely completed when gold was discovered 80 miles to the south on Orofino Creek, in 1860. But not until the 1880s, when gold was found in the streams feeding the Coeur d'Alene, did the rich mineral resources of the "billion-dollar triangle" begin to attract attention.

The district's fame began with the discovery of placer gold in 1881. By 1883 new towns were crowded with prospectors. Gold remained at about $20 an ounce in those days, the gold rush did not last long, and most of its boom towns soon died. They were replaced by the mining camps that grew up around the rich lodes of silver and lead. Noah Kellogg discovered the famous Bunker Hill-Sullivan mine in 1885, and the new town nearby was named for him. Soon afterward the Tiger and Poorman lead mines were located. Other great mines in the region include the Hecla, the Day, and the Star. In 1892 a mining war was fought, with miners pitted against owners (Smith 1961). By 1895 the district was established as one of the foremost lead and silver producers in North America.

The area has had a turbulent labor-management history. Even before mining was established, whites and Indians had to do some adjusting to each other's life styles, resulting in accommodation rather than armed conflict (Bischoff 1974). By the time immigrant laborers had come to work the mines from Wales and other northern European countries, managers distrusted workers, and an armed conflict broke out in 1892. This Coeur d'Alene mining war had at issue wages, which managers wanted to freeze at first and later to lower (Smith 1961; Magnuson 1968; and Harriman 1899). Union organizers from the Industrial Workers of the World (IWW) were tried but found not guilty in a famous court case in Boise, Idaho, with Clarence Darrow representing union men, for the murder of an ex-governor who had lead Idaho during that mining war. Later in the 1930s, Idaho passed a Criminal Syndicalism Act, designed specifically to outlaw the influence of persons who were threatening or involved with labor violence. Men went to prison, convicted under the act, and its constitutionality was tested, but it was not revoked from Idaho law. The act was effective in destroy-

1

ing the IWW, a strong union in Idaho and other states (Sims 1974). Labor troubles were evident also in the long winter strike of 1959-1960, in which a jurisdictional labor dispute was involved. Negotiation, union contracts, strikes, and arbitration are part and parcel of the ways of the miners of the Coeur d'Alene.

The Sunshine Mine was a rather late development. Claimed in 1884 by True and Dennis Blake, it was worked intermittently on a small scale for over thirty years. By 1909 the secretive "Blake boys" had completed ten tunnels, three open cuts, and a shaft. No one ever knew how much ore they mined. Estimates placed its total value at somewhere between a few thousand and a half-million dollars. The Blakes later leased their operation, and in 1921 the Sunshine Mining Company was incorporated (Hobson 1940:35-36). It became the richest silver mine in the nation. In 1971 it produced one-fifth of all the silver mined in the United States. It was also the largest single employer of miners in the Coeur d'Alene district.

Men go down the mine shafts on elevators called *skips*. Three shifts of workers keep the mine in operation around the clock. Trains take them along the tunnel to the *stopes*, where the ore is mined. What rock has been blasted the previous shift is wet drilled with a "Jack-leg" and loaded ("slushed into a chute") by a motorman from below into ore cars to go to the surface for smelting. Men are paid on a piecework or "gyppo" basis. In addition to miners, supporting personnel such as carpenters, electricians, and mechanics also work on every shift inside the mine.

The Sunshine Mine is a "hot mine," with temperatures over 100° much of the time. The miners sometimes work only thirty minutes at a stretch; longer periods may cause heat cramps. But despite the high temperatures, fires are infrequent in hard-rock mines. In thirty years there had been only three fires in the Kellogg area, one of which occurred in 1946 in the Sunshine Mine which killed no one but was severe enough to bring operations to a halt for six weeks (Roberts 1972a:12). Many of the miners accept the danger as part of the job. One said, "It's an old place, there's not much seepage, and those timbers are awfully dry. . . . We all understand the danger, that's something everyone knows. We just don't talk too much about it" (Roberts 1972a:12). Prior to the disaster, the Sunshine had experienced 46 industrial fatalities in its entire history (Griner 1973).

Fire in the Sunshine Mine

On the morning of May 2, 1972, fire broke out in the Sunshine Mine, over a half-mile below the earth's surface. The fire may have smouldered in an abandoned shaft a long time before flaring up that Tuesday morning. When it did explode, waves of smoke and carbon monoxide filled the tunnels.

There were 174 men in the mine. Eighty-one of them escaped quickly. Some just walked out. For others escape was a slow matter of crawling out of mine tunnels. Below the point where the fire was burning, the only escape route open was the Number 10 Shaft, and it was soon blocked by smoke and gas. The operator of the elevator hoist died while trying to get men out of the shaft.

Rescue efforts began immediately but were hampered by the smoke and heat. The fire was burning in an unused portion of the mine and was impossible to extinguish easily. Local mine administrators and state and federal mine officials rushed to the scene. Directed by mine officials, Sunshine Mine employees and workers from other local mines searched for the missing men.

Relatives waited at the mine entrance for word of a husband, brother, or father. Newsmen converged on the community, transmitting to national audience the days of frenzied activity, anguish, and finally, horror.

The fire started on Tuesday. That night there were five known dead, and seventy-seven missing. On Wednesday the bodies of nineteen others were discovered, and on Thursday eight more were found dead. Friday evening three more bodies were found, for a toll of thirty-five. At that point, mine officials said that forty-seven men were missing.

Rescue efforts continued over the weekend. After indications that some word about the missing men was imminent, a resurgence of fire and smoke from the mine slowed rescue operations and reduced the hope that there might be survivors. On Monday a check of company records revealed that nine additional men were missing—fifty-six were still left unaccounted for. Tuesday evening, May 9, the two survivors were found and brought out of the mine. They had managed to find a fresh-air source and had subsisted for the week on the lunches of their dead coworkers. Rescuers and the waiting families were jubilant, and hopes for the missing men soared. Wednesday night, eight days after the fire had broken out, forty men were still missing. The following day, their bodies were found. In all, ninety-one perished. Never in the history of the western United States had so many died in a mine disaster.

Three Types of Miners' Wives

By the end of the first day the fire had separated the miners' wives in the Kellogg area into three groups. First, there were those whose husbands were among the missing, those who already were widows, although many would not know that for certain for nine days. Second, there were the survivors' wives, whose attitudes and actions during the ensuing days reflected their good fortune. Through no action of their own, their husbands had been spared. (There is a folk motif, however, that some wives saved their husbands' lives by not getting them up for work!) Third, there were other wives whose husbands were miners for other companies. Their husbands had not been in hazard at the Sunshine, but they worked other mines, and disasters were possible there also. We shall refer to these three groups as the widows, the survivors' wives, and the other miners' wives.

This book is about the consequences of sudden widowhood; specifically how the Sunshine Mine widows adjusted to their losses, redefined their personal worlds, and changed their lives. In order that factors directly linked to widowhood might be kept separate from changes deriving from living in a community that experiences a sudden disaster, or from changes that follow a husband's losing many coworkers, information from wives of survivors and wives of men employed in nearby mines will also be presented.

The main source of information for these comparisons is a survey of the miners' wives and widows conducted in the Kellogg area in November 1972, six months after the fire. In all, 222 women were interviewed: 44 widows, 50 wives of survivors, and 128 wives of other miners. Details about the interviewing are given in the appendix. For now, it is enough to note that the average interview lasted about two and a half hours and that the interviewers were local women specially trained for this project. None of the interviewers were involved in the study as subjects, but since they were residents of the Coeur d'Alene Mining District, they had been affected emotionally by the disaster. Some had lost friends in the disaster; some had helped relief operations during the search for the missing men.

The interview schedule contained questions on women's backgrounds, their reactions to the disaster and activities during the rescue operations, patterns of involvement with family, friends, and community, changes in those patterns after the fire, and their life situations and outlook at the time of the interview.

The fire was seen differently by the widows, survivors' wives, and other wives. Presumably their predisaster behavior was similar, but when the identity of the trapped men was known, the wives of the trapped men were defined as potential, and later probably, widows, and the survivors' wives as very fortunate that their men had escaped. Naturally wives whose men worked other mines may also have felt "there but for the grace of God . . . ," but their own husbands had not just experienced an immediate brush with death, and this difference in circumstances was bound to have an effect on their attitudes about the disaster. It is therefore not surprising that following the diaster, the three groups of wives differed in their ideas about who was to blame, the nature and need for aid to victims' families, and about mining as an occupation.

Initial Reactions to News of the Fire

Mining communities are supposed to be better prepared than other communities for disaster or serious trouble. Sometimes mining accidents occur so frequently that communities learn to anticipate the stress of unexpected crises and accidents (Lang and Lang 1964). Among coal miners, it is reported, "The daily threat of death to the breadwinner affected the families of the miners. Many wives stated that as they saw their husbands off to work, they wondered if they would see them alive again" (Lucas 1969:10).

Kellogg was not a community that anticipated this disaster. Although accidents in hard-rock mining occur, fatalities are not common, and a fire like this was unknown. A few of the women could remember fatal accidents involving either their own relatives or their husband's male relatives (9 percent recalled fatalities among their own relatives, and 7 percent for husbands'). This is despite the fact that high proportions of kin on both sides of the women's families had long experience in mining: of the total sample, 72 percent said one or more of the husband's close male relatives had worked in a mine, and 57 percent had close male relatives of their own who were or had been miners. Although the women had known miners and mining over long periods in both their own and in their husbands' families, they had little familiarity with fatal mining accidents, and nothing to prepare them for sudden, large-scale mortality among their men.

This lack of precedent for a major disaster can explain the mildness of their first reactions to news of trouble at the Sunshine Mine (table 1-1). Of the widows, 44 percent said that at first they "didn't think it was serious," as compared to 34 percent of the survivors' wives and 28 percent of the other miners' wives. In fact, initial shock or surprise was noted twice as often by the other groups than by the widows, which may have been related to the fact that the other wives heard of the fire later in the day.

One woman who did not think it was serious at first said she thought, "So there's a fire. He's helping put it out." Another said she was calm because she did not think a hard-rock mine fire could be serious. One learned her husband's mining partner was out of the mine and so thought her husband was outside fighting it: "I thought it was an outside fire." Another was working and did not worry at first: "No one called me so I assumed he got out. My brother went up and found that he [her husband] was still underground. I was scared, but not really worried." Still another widow said, "I thought he'd come out. He might have to be at the hospital for smoke inhalation but nothing more. He'd been in two fires before and got out, so I figured he'd get out this time."

Table 1-1
Wives' Reports of Their First Reactions to News that There Was Trouble at the Sunshine Mine

First Reaction	Widows (%)	Survivors' Wives (%)	Other Miners' Wives (%)
Could not believe it, shock, or surprise	14	28	31
Panicked, concerned, or worried	12	20	27
Did not think it serious	44	34	28
Other	30	18	14
Total	100	100	100
(N)	(43)	(50)	(128)

Women who said they expressed disbelief, shock, or surprise referred to the supposed safety of hard-rock mines from fires. One said, "I couldn't believe it. This doesn't happen in a silver mine." Widows who classified themselves as "panicked, concerned, or worried" told about their reactions:

> I was shook, scared. I drove to the mine immediately. I knew it was worse than they said it was. Friends told me they had seen him O.K. I was rummy [sic] but I couldn't cry.

> I was working; I came home and didn't say anything. I kept running. . . . I went to the mine to the Shifter's Shack at 4:00. I found out there that he was dead. His brother told me at the mine.

Finally there were responses classified as "other." One picked up her children and drove to the mine: "I thought they'd be out before we got there." Another was prepared for the worst: "My husband always said if they had a fire, there wouldn't be any air. After just 108 got out, I had no hope." (The news media at first reported 108, but it was later discovered that 81 escaped at first.) Another response: "My husband is never late. I got supper and he wasn't home. Friends came and said a lot of men were trapped. I didn't really react."

Once people heard about the fire, about half of the subjects talked to someone about the news, primarily by telephone. Most who did contact someone talked to immediate family members or in-laws. There was little difference among the three groups of women in this pattern.

The widows, however, had one distinguishing characteristic in their initial pattern of communication. They were more likely to contact a reliable source to confirm the news of trouble at the mine. Half of them contacted an authoritative source, compared to only one in eight of the survivors' wives and other miners' wives. The Sunshine Mining Company was the source most frequently sought. Survivors' wives had little need to seek authoritative word because their husbands either came home or telephoned, but the widowed received no official word. Wives of miners employed elsewhere, less directly involved, probably waited for confirmation via friends or the mass media.

Some of the widows who went to the mine seeking news of their men were told to go home because no one knew how bad the fire was. Some were not allowed access to the mine entrance. In retrospect some of the initial communications from the mine were needlessly cruel. One widow said she telephoned at 3:00 p.m. and was told, "There is a fire, no casualities, no danger, no one trapped." Another remembered, "At first I was told nothing. They they said, 'Yes, there is a fire, and some men are trapped.'" After several calls to the mine a wife was told that mine officials did not know who had left, and the widow remembers wondering if the escaped men were able to call or if they did not have time.

Some wives contacted their husbands' supervisors or fellow workers:

> I called the shift boss to see if he was home. He wasn't home. I called a friend on a different shift to see what he knew. They tried to reassure me—they didn't know if they should tell me but they wouldn't let the night shift come on. I was told he was still at work, but the shift was over. Sometimes guys stop at a bar.

Others responded to rumors of injury by telephoning the hospital. One widow heard that there had been a bus taken to the hospital.

Repeated again and again in statements about the first day were feelings of confidence and assurance: "He wasn't in any danger because he knew the mine inside out." Finally, some made no attempts to confirm the reports: "My husband left me here to tend his children—that's what I am doing."

Initially, then, the miners' wives were unprepared for a disaster. When they first heard of it, they were concerned but typically optimistic. About half of them began to contact families by telephone, and half contacted an authoritative source to confirm the news.

Emergent Activity Patterns
During the Week of the Search

During periods of disaster old social patterns may break down. New and unexpected situations change the social context, and old definitions and forms may be irrelevant. Sociologists refer to patterns of expected behavior as "norms," and when crisis interrupts usual behaviors, new norms emerge (Turner 1964). Of course, many prior social patterns continue in force during a disaster, and general predispositions—"do *something*, even if it's wrong"—maintain their influence. During the week's search for the missing men, several types of patterned behavior evolved, and sometimes there was social pressure in support of the emergent norms.

Waiting at the Mine Site

During the week of search the mine site took on aspects of hallowed ground, and three-fourths of the widows-to-be made one or more pilgrimages there (see table 1-2). The men had disappeared into the ground there, and for some, just being nearby and available was better than waiting elsewhere. Nearly one-third of the widows who visited the mine did so immediately, another third went within a few hours of hearing about the fire, and another third went the next day. When asked why they went, 10 percent said they went to pick up their husbands from work. The others said they

Table 1-2
Activities during the Week-long Search for the Missing Men

Activity	Widows (%)	Survivors' Wives (%)	Other Miners' Wives (%)
Went to mine site sometime	77	56	26
Male member of family involved in search	32	62	31
Participated in organized assistance	9	21	36
Participated in informal assistance	56	72	69
Total cases (N)	(44)	(50)	(128)

went primarily to wait for information. Some stayed only briefly; a few waited the whole week; the majority shuttled back and forth between home and the mine.

Half of the widows in the sample said they preferred to wait at the mine site. Some felt serious stress, wanting to be home with the children but also wanting to be as close to the husband as possible. Others said that there was not much to gain by waiting at the mine but felt staying there preferable to sitting at home and worrying.

The other half of the widows were critical of people who waited at the mine. In part they may have been reducing their own uneasiness for not participating in the vigil at the mine, and in part their attitudes may have reflected a realistic appraisal of the situation. It would make no difference in the safety of their men whether they came to the mine or not. They stayed away, and they responded to perceived social pressure with comments about the futility of waiting at the mine. There was "nothing for them [widows] to gain—they were just in the way," they said, and "they should have stayed home with their children."

One who waited three days and nights said she stayed so that she could be there to ride to the hospital with her husband. A woman whose vigil lasted all eight days said she did not have a phone. "I thought we could see them coming out. I didn't want to come home; the children were taken care of. By Friday (three days) they told us most were dead." Nevertheless, she waited at the mine five more days. For some the waiting took on aspects of denial and suffering that characterize a religious fast or the initial part of a "rite-of-passage" ritual, with its "obsessive-compulsive" aspects:

> I couldn't go to work every day and know my husband was down in the mine. My responsibilities at the job weren't as important as a woman who had children. I sat in the car [seven days] alone outside the [mine] gate. I woke up every morning in my car and nothing had changed.

The emergent norm that the appropriate behavior for a wife whose husband was missing was to wait at the mine exacted its greatest toll upon mothers of young children. Whether they stayed home or waited at the mine, they felt guilty about neglecting someone. Then too there was the strength in numbers that came from being with others who also waited. At home the grief and loss must be borne alone; at the mine one could be part of a visible community who share the same plight. "My children begged me to stay home when I went home," said one young mother, but while waiting at the mine, "I felt like I wasn't the only person." The norm that waiting at the mine was expected of one, that it was what one *ought* to do, was expressed by several:

> We all felt we *should* [emphasis added] be there to wait for our husbands. I
> wanted to know everything that was happening. I stayed the whole time at
> the mine except to shower at home. I felt closer to him at the mine site. At
> home I feared I'd worry too much, though folks wanted me to stay home.

But waiting had its psychic costs, and some found the tension easier to bear
away from the mine. A wife waited two days at the mine and then was
talked into leaving by relatives: "I felt better at a friend's house."

Those who did not wait at the mine justified their actions in ways that
showed they had felt social pressure but had resisted the emergent norm. "I
had no right to put my children through going to the mine," said one
mother, "I wanted to be near the children when they heard so many uglies
at school."

Several had to pick up the family car at the mine but did not stay. One
asked a few questions but left after twenty minutes: "I couldn't do it. But
it's personal. It would have been torture to sit there and wait." Another
finally went to the mine to see if one of the bodies brought up was her husband, but she did not wait there: "It wasn't doing them any good. They
could have accomplished more at home." And some stayed home because
they felt it would upset their children more to have both parents gone or
because they felt that if there were news, it would reach them more effi-
ciently if they were at home near the telephone: "It would have been difficult to find me in the mess at the mine site." Besides, some found the
presence of the crowd unsettling, not supportive: "I didn't want to be
around people who were hysterical like myself."

Doing Something to Help

A second norm that quickly emerged was that people and organizations
should "do something." Even the wives of the missing men, who themselves needed assistance, contributed to the effort. Although the fire was
without precedent, community response was swift. The kinds of things people could do to help were different for men than for women. Immediately
an official search for the missing men was begun, with the assistance of
federal and state mine inspectors, paid employees of the Sunshine, and
volunteers from the community. In about one-third of the families of the
widows and other miners' wives, male family members were directly involved in the search. Among the survivors' wives, whose husbands were all
employees of the Sunshine Mine, the proportion was twice as high.

Women who were unable to participate directly in the search helped in-
formally and supported efforts by various organizations. As the percentages in table 1-2 reveal, over half the widows did things to help other
families in similar circumstances. Involvement in informal helping activities

was even higher among the other women in the community. Informal help, primarily visiting or comforting, baby-sitting, or sending food or flowers, was reported by about 70 percent of the wives whose husbands were not among the missing. Participation in organized assistance (Red Cross or church groups) was infrequent on the part of the widows but more common in the other groups. One third of the other miners' wives and one-fifth of the survivors' wives helped in organized assistance efforts.

Many widows mentioned help at the mine site. "I tried to cheer up the other ladies. It was kind of appreciated. They were so worried about their husbands that they cheered me too." Another said, "I visited and talked to a few women we knew as a couple." One widow who did not give aid said, "I didn't help because I couldn't even take care of myself."

The type of formal assistance most often reported by the widows was church-sponsored help (70 percent) and almost as frequent (61 percent) was aid from the Red Cross. Forty-one percent of the widows reported receiving the assistance of someone from the clergy. When asked to evaluate the aid they had received, four out of five widows said that community support was excellent; moreover, almost everyone who gave aid felt that it was appreciated. Both the givers and receivers of aid thus seem to have been satisfied with the nature and amount of aid during the week of the fire.

Immediate Personal Reactions

Some ideas about the immediate personal impact of the disaster may be gleaned from statements by journalists who were there. These insights from journalists will be supplemented with our subjects' reports of their own reactions to the crisis. The questionable validity of their recollections about attitudes and feelings six months after the fact is admitted. It is probable that the ambiguities inherent in an unfamiliar set of experiences and emotions will have been reduced in the interviewing period between the fire and our interview, and that a reshaping and redefining of attitudes will occur as the widow develops a more or less coherent mental picture of what happened to her and how she felt and acted. But this is a situation in which data of uncertain accuracy are better than none at all. The journalists whose immediate accounts make news bring the biases of personal and professional experience to their task; the women who experienced the disaster, perhaps more reliable than the reporters because they are telling their own stories, have a different set of blind spots and selective perceptions.

Questions in the interview schedule about personal reactions included a general query about how the women felt most of the time during the week of search and waiting, as well as a list of specific types of emotional response (depression, anxiety, anger) to which they answered yes or no.

The widows' most frequent self-description involved a sense of being numb or in shock. The same terminology was used by the journalists who told of the community's reactions. The waiting women were described in press accounts as numb, stonefaced, crying, exhausted, their faces "set hard and white." But despite feelings of numbness, the widows' reports about their specific reactions and behavior do not show them as inept or withdrawn. Most were able to carry on necessary activities. Some did know immediately that their husbands had died, and others learned during the week. All were thus not subject to a week of hope and fear for their men.

As the week progressed the vigil at the mine site settled into a regular pattern:

> It became a familiar routine.
> A mother would leave to do the family chores, to tend to younger children. She would be replaced by a grown daughter, or another relative waiting to snatch any bit of news.
> The women were dressed against the chill and many appeared to be in their Sunday best, conservative and staid. . . .
> Some of the women were praying. Others sat with their heads down, totally exhausted. A few yards away, in a makeshift room converted from a parts warehouse, some of the older women waited ("Kellogg Women Stand Vigil, Hoping" 1972:1).

On Sunday interdenominational services were held in the mine's machine shop, and the prayers and hymns combined with the sounds of working metal.

Ministers had requested that waiting relatives wear a tag with the miner's name on it so that they could be located in the crowd should there be some word about a man. The reaction of Mrs. Myrna Flory, whose husband was later rescued, illustrates the countervailing pressures the women faced. On the one hand, they were afraid of news, afraid that when it came, it would be bad. On the other hand, the ambiguity left them suspended, unmoored, and was itself psychologically punishing. Mrs. Flory refused to wear the tag: "I don't think I could take it if they came over and told me he was dead," she said; "I only want them to tell me if he's alive." A moment later, though, she reversed herself: "I wish they'd get them up, dead or alive," she said; "I don't think people can take it any longer" (Roberts 1972c:32). Another of the waiting wives responded to the uncertainty and tension by affirming that her husband was all right: "I know he's all right. . . . If I didn't think he was, I'd go off the deep end. I wonder what my husband is thinking about, down there in the dark, hungry and cold" (Roberts 1972b:13).

The frequent optimistic reports, followed by the stark reality, added to the deep frustration. "They keep getting our hopes up and stuff, they give us a time when they'll know something and then they let us down,'' said one; "How much can people take? They're getting near hysteria over there.'' Another said, "We sit and sit. They tell us the death count is 10, then 24, then 27. Why don't they get their story straight? The fretting and worrying is getting to us'' (Roberts 1972c:32).

But along with talk of "going off the deep end,'' and the judgments that people could not take it any more, were the assurances that the collective endurance was sufficient for survival whatever the final outcome might be:

> The men who work in each mine in this rugged country are a clan, a large family united by the bond of danger. And in a time of tragedy, the bonds tighten. People cling to each other—hands touch, arms drape over shoulders. As one wife put it, "There are no strangers here'' (Roberts 1972c:32).

In part, the wives echoed this affirmation of community spirit to our interviewers. Almost everyone said they needed to talk to others about the fire (table 1-3). This need to communicate was most strongly felt by the other miners' wives, and least often reported by the widows (percentages reporting the felt need to talk were, respectively, 90 percent, 78 percent, and 67 percent). Even when they did not want to talk about the fire, the situation sometimes demanded it. "My home was Grand Central Station,'' said one woman. "How could you help it?''

Other indications of community solidarity were the women's responses to questions about whether they felt isolated from family and friends or from the community in general during the week. Only 5 percent of the other miners' wives, 14 percent of the survivors wives, and 12 percent of the widows said they felt isolated from family. Figures for isolation from the community, respectively, were 9 percent of the other miners' wives (their most frequently stated reason for the feelings of isolation was that "everything in town was at a standstill''), 2 percent for the survivors' wives, and 9 percent for the widows. A widow who did feel isolated was alone in a crowd: "Forty-two of my husband's relatives showed up. I never knew any of them before, and I felt a stranger in my own home. *None* of them stayed for the funeral.'' Another said, "I didn't want to be around anybody. I still feel that way. I want to think my own thoughts.''

Behind the assertions of community solidarity and "no strangers here'' attitudes were some strains of hostility, avoidance, and recrimination. Almost everyone said they felt helpless; and yet about two thirds of these subjects said they were able to reduce their feelings of helplessness by keeping busy, caring for children, praying, helping, and being with others. But those most in need of support—the widows and widows-to-be—were al-

Table 1-3
Proportions of Women Reporting Particular Emotional Reactions during the Search for the Missing Men

Yes Response To:	Widows	Survivors' Wives	Other Miners' Wives
Anxiety	98	96	97
Praying	91	86	89
Crying	86	74	69
Helplessness	88	92	94
Frustration	79	86	74
Difficulty in accepting reality	79	68	75
Depression	70	82	77
Difficulty in organizing thoughts	67	60	50
Need to talk to others about fire	67	78	90[a]
Resentment or hostility	55	45	31[a]
Inability in decision making	51	34	20[a]
Difficulty in responding to family needs	42	22	11[a]
Felt uncomfortable around anyone	39	30	28
Anger	38	45	32
Difficulty in maintaining self-control	37	42	30
Difficulty acting constructively	37	39	23[a]
Felt isolated from family	12	14	5
Total cases (N)	(44)	(50)	(128)

[a]Differences among the three samples are statistically significant at the .05 level (Chi-square test).

ready stigmatized by their loss, and some women found it uncomfortable to associate with them. Between one fourth and one fifth of the other women said they felt uncomfortable around the wives and mothers of the missing men. The most commonly expressed reasons for this discomfort were that they did not know what to say to the widows, that they knew there was no hope, or that the knowledge that her own husband was alive and safe made her uneasy in dealing with others who had lost, or probably would lose, their husbands. Thirty-nine percent of the widows also reported feeling uncomfortable around others during the week, but there was little agreement about which people made them uncomfortable. Some were uneasy around relatives, around other widows, around visitors, or, in two cases, around everyone.

One widow who reported feeling uncomfortable said, "Visitors stayed too long. I'm not too emotional, so I kept it all inside because I couldn't express my feelings in their presence." The disaster called forth hypocrisy in some, and that made widows uncomfortable. One had negative feelings about her father-in-law "because he showed he loved his son—but it was phony because he didn't really." Another felt uncomfortable around some "smart-aleck guys who said they ran when they heard about the fire. One guy said he wanted to get rid of my husband so he could have me." The interviewer noted at the end of that schedule that "this woman loved and appreciated her man."

There were also undercurrents of resentment and hostility, usually directed at the management of the Sunshine. Not surprisingly, the women who had lost the most were most bitter. Fifty-five percent of the widows reported feelings of hostility, compared to 45 and 31 percent of the survivors' and other miners' wives.

Reacting to a checklist of specific emotional reactions (see table 1-3), over 95 percent of subjects in all three groups noted anxiety as a personal attribute during the week of search for the missing men. Next to anxiety in frequency was a "need to pray," reported by over 85 percent of the women.

Of all the emotional responses listed in table 1-3, five of them show differences among the three groups of wives that are unlikely to be due to chance. Compared to the other women, the widows cried more, felt more resentment or hostility, were less able to make decisions, had more difficulty in responding to family needs, and said they had more difficulty acting constructively. Widows also had less need to talk to others about the fire.

Physiological reactions are a manifestation of emotional response and are very common among residents of commnities experiencing serious crises or disasters. Among the present subjects, physical reactions (typically insomnia, loss of appetite, headaches, or combinations of these) were reported by 80 percent of the widows, 62 percent of survivors' wives, and 59 percent of the other miners' wives. Women also reported physical disturbances of other family members. Three fourths of both widows and survivors' wives said that members of their families had physical disturbances. So did 43 percent of the survivors' wives.

Reactions to News-media Personnel

Another aspect of the week of waiting was the influx of news-media personnel into the community. Reporters and camera people from major news networks questioned mine officials, the victims' families, and even covered funerals of victims whose bodies were discovered early in the week. It was reported in the media that community reaction to the press was hostile, and to check this report, the interview schedule included some questions about women's contact with and reaction to the press personnel. We anticipated that of the three types of women, the widows would have the most contact with the press and presumably would have been the most hostile.

The women's responses to interviewers in the present study corroborated the news reports of community hostility toward the press corps. Answers to the question, "What was your first reaction to the arrival of the press corps?" showed that if neutral responses such as "I expected them" or "they were just doing their job" are combined with the pro-media responses, sharp differences emerge among the three groups of women.

The widows were least likely to have a neutral or favorable impression of the press, followed by the other two groups. Two thirds of the other miners' wives, compared to half of the survivors' wives and only about one third of the widows had essentially positive or neutral reactions to the newsmen. About one fourth of the widows and survivors' wives said they "couldn't stand them here," or reported the newsmen were in the way, were too nosy, or upset people.

Actual contact with the press was most frequent among the widows, although less than half came into direct contact. Women who had direct contact were more hostile toward the press than those without direct contact.

One widow's experiences are worth illustrating although they were not typical. She lived close to the mine, and news personnel often stopped at her home to use the telephone. She therefore had the stress of dealing with her husband plus the added burden of a steady stream of news personnel.

Summary

Fire in the Sunshine Mine in Northern Idaho on May 2, 1972, trapped 93 miners. It took a week to reach the trapped men; in the interim the community waited in anguish, wondering if the men were alive. Finally the smoke cleared enough to allow rescurers to reach the workers, and two were saved. The remaining 91 died. This book is about the women who were widowed by the fire. Their reactions are compared to those of the survivors' wives, women whose husbands were in the Sunshine at the time of the fire but who escaped, and to other miners' wives.

Even though most of these women had miners in their families, prior contact with death was present for fewer than 10 percent. Reaction to initial news of the fire was therefore that it was "not serious." If widows-to-be did contact the Sunshine Mine, the messages were contradictory and also minimized danger.

The fire and the uncertainty of the fate of the trapped men created an unusual social situation in the community. There were new pressures, and patterns evolved to deal with these new strains. Waiting at the mine site was an emergent activity about which women had to decide and justify. Another emergent activity was the need to do something "to help," and dealing with the "helpful" actions of others.

Personal reactions as recalled by our subjects six months after the fire as well as those collected by journalists emphasize numbness and shock and anxiety. The traumas of waiting, hearing rumors, and being targets for journalists' interviews added to these womens' burdens.

In contrast to the indifference or outright hostility toward news personnel was the avid following of the press coverage of the disaster. All of the other miners' wives read, listened, or watched news of the disaster as did 95 percent of the widows and 90 percent of the survivors' wives. Almost everyone read the local newspaper as well as followed development via television, radio, and other newspapers. A majority of the women said they felt that the press coverage was important to their understanding of the disaster, although the widows and survivors' wives were less likely to say this (73 percent and 62 percent, respectively) than the other miners' wives (87 percent). One widow said that she "found things out from the news long before officials told us at the mine."

In sum, women's reactions to the reporters were far more negative than their attitudes about the news as reported. In general, the subjects followed the news closely and seemed to think that the press coverage was beneficial. The dilemma faced by the press was to maintain coverage and still not give the impression of being in the way or being "too nosy." Obviously they were not successful in resolving this dilemma to the satisfaction of the widows and survivors' wives.

References

Bischoff, William N. 1974. "The Coeur d'Alene Country, 1805-1892." In *Interior Salish and Eastern Washington Indians I*, ed. Stuart A. Chalfant, pp. 197-296. New York: Garland.

Griner, Carl. 1973. Idaho State Inspector of Mines. Personal interview by Carol D.H. Harvey, January.

Harriman, Job. 1899. *The Class War in Idaho: The Horrors of the Bull Pen*. Facsimile reproduction in 1965 by the Shorey Book Store, Seattle, Wa.

Hobson, George C. 1940. *Gems of Thought and History of Shoshone County*. Kellogg, Idaho: Kellogg Evening News Press, pp. 35-36.

"Kellogg Women Stand Vigil, Hoping." 1972. *Salt Lake Tribune*, May 4, p. 1. Reprinted by permission.

Lang, Kurt, and Lang, Gladys Engel. 1964. "Collective Responses to the Threat of Disaster." In *The Threat of Impending Disaster*, ed. G.H. Grosser, H. Wechsler, and M. Greenblatt, pp. 58-75. Cambridge, Mass.: MIT Press.

Lucas, Rex A. 1969. *Men in Crisis: A Study of a Mine Disaster*. New York: Basic Books, p. 10.

Magnuson, Richard G. 1968. *Coeur d'Alene Diary: The First Ten Years of Harrock Mining in North Idaho*. Portland, Oreg.: Metropolitan Press.

Roberts, Steven V. 1972*a*. "Rescuers Strive to Save 58 Trapped by Fire Deep in Silver Mine." *New York Times*, May 4, p. 12. © 1972 by The New York Times Company. Reprinted by permission.

_____. 1972*b*. "Death Toll is Now 32 in Silver Mine Fire." *New York Times*, May 5, p. 13. © 1972 by The New York Times Company. Reprinted by permission.

_____ . 1972*c*. "Waiting is Endless for Relatives at Silver Mine." *New York Times*, May 6, p. 32. © 1972 by The New York Times Company. Reprinted by permission.

Sims, Robert C. 1974. "Idaho's Criminal Syndicalism Act: One State's Response to Radical Labor." *Labor History*, 15 (no. 4) Fall:511-527.

Smith, Robert Wayne. 1961. *The Coeur d'Alene Mining War of 1892*. Corvallis, Oreg.: Oregon State College Press.

Turner, Ralph H. 1964. "Collective Behavior." In *Handbook of Modern Sociology*, ed. R.E.L. Faris, pp. 382-425. Chicago: Rand McNalley.

2 Differences before the Fire

Our major concern is with differences among the widows, survivors' wives, and other women in attitudes, definitions, and reported behaviors following the fire. Presumably consideration of these differences will help us to understand aspects of adjustment to sudden widowhood. Before it can be established that differences among the three groups mean anything, we must know how they differed, if at all, prior to the fire. Accordingly it will be necessary to compare the groups on background factors such as age, income, education, and religion, as well as characteristics of family structure such as family size and maternal employment. The women's personal characteristics such as age, education, and religion may be distinguished from attributes of the family such as family income and family size. Each of these types of "background" will be treated separately.

Personal Characteristics of the Women

Age

The widows were neither older nor younger than the women in the other groups. In response to the instruction, "Will you please look at the card and tell me into which bracket your age falls?", 56 percent of them noted a category in the 20-39 range, compared to 54 percent of the survivors' wives and 62 percent of the other miners' wives. In each sample the median fell on the age 35-39 category. Of course these widows are far younger than widows generally, whose median age at widowhood is reported to be 56 (Lopata 1973:100). It should be noted that there is a wide range of ages in all three groups, from under 20 to over 65. The widows share the characteristic that they lost their husbands at the same time, but by then some had been married for decades while others were almost newlyweds.

Education

The widows ranged in educational attainment from "some grade school" for one respondent to "college graduate" for four widows. Forty-five percent of them said they had completed "some high school," and 34 percent were high school graduates. For some reason, the widows were less well-educated than the other women: 52 percent of the survivors' wives and 48 percent of the other miners' wives were high school graduates. In comparison to the general population of women in the United States, the educational attainment of all three groups was low: In 1972 white females in the United States aged 25 and over had a median educational attainment of 12.3 years (*Statistical Abstract of the United States*, 1973:115).

We are not able to explain the differences in education among the three groups. One possible explanation for the lower education of the widows is that their husbands, also being somewhat less educated than the average in the area, were more apt to be working in the high-risk jobs and thus were more apt to be lost in a mine fire. This explanation rests on at least two assumptions. First, the educational attainment of the men is congruent with that of their wives, and second, the men with lower attainment were in fact more likely to die in the fire. Neither of these assumptions was borne out by data. Although the widows are less educated than the survivors' wives, that differential does not appear when their husbands are compared. In fact, the survivors and victims of the fire had almost exactly the same number of years of schooling. If anything, the victims were slightly better educated; 52 percent of them had graduated from high school, compared to 44 percent of the survivors and 48 percent of the other miners. A greater risk on the part of the less-educated husbands does not explain the educational differences between the widows and the other women; other explanations are unknown.

Religion

About three fifths of the widows and the other miners' wives said they belonged to a church, whereas survivors' wives were less apt to claim church membership (42 percent, compared to 62 percent for the other miners' wives). There are also some differences in denominational affiliation among the three groups of women. We are not sure what these differences mean, but since we will be comparing the groups, it may be important to note them. (It should be remembered that the percentages to be compared are based on fairly small numbers of women. When the women reporting no affiliation were removed, the numbers left that formed the base for the contrasts in type of denomination were 25 widows, 19 survivors' wives, and 77 other miners' wives. With such small samples only fairly large differences are meaningful.)

Other miners' wives who were Catholics were about twice as frequent as among widows and survivors' wives; the proportions were 29 percent compared to 16 percent for both widows and survivors' wives. Protestants made up approximately the same proportion in all three samples, ranging from 65 percent among the other miners' wives to 72 percent among the survivors' wives. There was some minor variation by type of Protestantism; a slim minority (up to 15 percent for survivors' wives and less frequent for the others) were Mormon, a conservative religious group.

Apparently something about the nature of the work, the hiring processes, the history of the work force of the Sunshine Mine, or about the sample made its people slightly different in religious composition from that of the other miners in the region; the wives of Sunshine Mine employees, that is, both widows and survivors' wives, are more apt to represent conservative or fundamentalist Protestant denominations, while among other miners' wives, the Roman Catholic and less conservative Protestant denominations are more typical.

Family Background

Another relevant factor of personal background is the status of the family in which these women were raised. Twenty-eight percent of the widows came from families in which the father was a miner, compared to 19 percent of the survivors' wives and 36 percent of the other miners' wives. The three groups of women did not differ, however, in the occupational status of their fathers. Approximately the same proportion (between 10 and 13 percent) came from homes where the father was a white collar or a professional worker. Another indicator of parents' social status is fathers' education, and here again the three samples are congruent: between two thirds and four fifths (survivors' wives) of them came from families in which the father had not completed high school.

The educational level of these women's mothers is interesting. Fully one fourth of the widows could not recall their mothers' educations, and we surmise that either it was not important to their daughters' perceptions or that the daughters were upset enough at the time of the interview that they could not recall such information clearly. (Comparable figures for the other two groups were 6 percent for survivors' wives and 14 percent for other miners' wives.) At any rate, from one third to 45 percent of the mothers of Idaho women surveyed had grade school or less education. (One mother did not attend school at all.) From 29 percent of widows' mothers up to 42 percent of survivors' wives' mothers attended or completed high school. Eleven percent of widows' mothers, 16 percent of survivors' wives' mothers, and 8 percent of the other miners' wives' mothers attended or graduated from college or a technical specialty school beyond high school. Mothers and fathers of these women, in general, had comparable educational levels.

Family Attributes

Income

The women were asked to approximate their family incomes in the year before the fire (1971) and to estimate their annual incomes for the present year (1972). The ten fixed-response categories ranged from a low of $1,000 to $2,999 to a high of $19,000 and over. The women's responses are summarized on table 2-1, which reveals substantial differences among the three groups in family incomes for 1971.

The widows reported higher 1971 incomes than did the other women. Only one fifth of them reported 1971 incomes under $9,000 compared to more than one third of the other women. Differences are even more striking at the upper end of the scale: twenty eight percent of the widows reported family incomes for the previous year at $13,000 or more compared to 4 percent of the survivors' wives and 14 percent of the other miners' wives (table 2-1).

The effects of the fire are apparent in the lower panel of table 2-1. Observe that the incomes for the families of widows and survivors are much lower than for the previous year. The Sunshine Mine was closed down for several months after the fire, and thus the projected incomes reflect that survivors had to find *temporary* work and did not succeed in finding work that paid as well as the Sunshine Mine.

The net effect of the decline of family income among the widows and survivors is to decrease the differences in income among the three groups in

Table 2-1
Family Income, 1971 and 1972 (Estimated), for Widows, Survivors' Wives, and Other Miners' Wives

Income	Widows	Survivors' Wives	Other Miners' Wives
1971[a]			
Under $9,000	21	36	36
$9,000-10,999	35	36	30
$11,000-12,999	16	24	21
$13,000 +	28	4	14
(N)	(43)	(50)	(125)
1972[a]			
Under $9,000	64	50	40
$9,000-10,999	19	20	26
$11,000-12,999	7	24	20
$13,000 +	10	6	14
(N)	(43)	(50)	(125)

[a]Interviews were conducted in November 1972, but respondents were asked about their family incomes for the entire calendar year.

1972. The families of widows and survivors made less money in 1972 than the other miners' wives, but even with the closing of the mine, the differences are not very large. The loss in family income is most apparent for the widows; three times as many of them expected family incomes under $9,000 in 1972 as compared to 1971.

Remarriage

The widows differed from the other women in their past experience with marital dissolution. Half of them had been married before, compared to only 28 percent of the survivors' wives and 30 percent of the other miners' wives. Three of the 44 widows had been widowed before and nineteen (43 percent) had been divorced. In contrast, only one of the 50 survivors' wives had been widowed, and 9 of the 125 other miners' wives who answered the question had been widowed. Percentages who had been divorced among these last two groups were 27 for survivors' wives and 22 percent for other miners' wives. The burden of the disaster seems to have fallen most heavily on women who had already experienced unusually high rates of marital dissolution.

Employment Status

Wives whose husbands were employed at the Sunshine Mine were somewhat more likely to work outside the home than were other miners' wives. Twenty-two percent of the widows and 20 percent of the survivors' wives were working outside the home before the fire, compared to 13 percent of the other miners' wives.

Some contrast with national statistics on women's employment may be of interest. In 1972, 44 percent of the total female population was employed for wages outside the home. Women ages 20 to 64 who were widowed, divorced, or married with husband absent had even higher rates of employment, with the figures for various age groups running at 60 percent or more employed for wages (*Statistical Abstracts of the United States*, 1973:221-222). The women of the Kellogg community were thus much less likely than their average American sisters to be employed for wages.

Children

The widows were slightly less likely to have children than the women in the other samples. Ninety-one percent of them had one or more children, compared to 96 percent of the survivors' wives and 98 percent of the other miners' wives. The widows who did have children were apt to have had more of them than were the other women. Only 28 percent of the widows had one or two children compared to 44 and 46 percent of the survivors' and other miners' wives; and yet, 31 percent of the widows had families of five or more children, compared to 20 percent of the survivors' wives and 16 percent of the other miners' wives. The average (mean) number of children for the widows was 3.4, compared to 2.9 for both comparison samples, and the differences are larger if the average number of children for mothers having *any* children are compared (3.7 for widows versus 3.0 for the other two groups).

Although the widows tended to have slightly larger families, they did not differ from the women in the other samples in ages of children; about three fifths of each sample had children under 21 living at home.

The Marriage Remembered

Because in subsequent chapters we will be concerned with reported changes in attitudes, interpersonal relationships, and formal affiliations following widowhood, it seems appropriate to conclude this brief review of predisaster differences among the three groups with a discussion of responses to four questions reflecting the perceived quality of the marital relationship. Differences between the widows and the other two groups of women in response to these questions are difficult to interpret because the widows are reporting about their marriages as they remember them. The questions were necessarily put in the past tense and perhaps they are likely to idealize the relationship now that their husbands are dead. In contrast, the survivors' wives and other miners' wives are reporting marriages as they exist at the present time.

When asked, "How frequently do (did) you and your husband discuss your problems? That is, do (did) you discuss your problems with your husband often, once in a while, rarely, or never?", between 66 and 69 percent of all three samples answered, "very often." The similarity among the three groups suggests that, on this item at least, the widows are not idealizing their marriages.

The same high congruity among samples appeared with respect to questions about husbands' reactions to wives' problems and about how close a companionship existed between the two. Between 74 and 77 percent of the women in all three samples responded that their husbands always or usually gave all the help they could when reacting to the wives' problems. Between 73 percent (other miner's wives) and 82 percent (widows) responded "very close" when asked, "How close of a personal friend or companion do you feel your husband is (was) to you?" There is some evidence of the idealization of the marital relationship in widows' responses to questions about how well they got along with their husbands. For example, in response to the question, "Some husbands react to their wives' problems by helping very little and others help a lot. Would you say your husband never, rarely, sometimes, usually, or always helps (helped) with your problems?", between 44 and 47 percent of the survivors' wives and the other miners' wives reported that husbands "always helped" when the wife has a problem, but among the widows 58 percent said their husbands "always helped."

A differential in favor of the absent husbands of the widows appears with respect to family decision making. In retrospect, the husbands of the widows seemed to have been a more dominant force in the family than are the living husbands in the comparison samples. In one fifth of the families of the survivors' wives and other miners' wives, husbands are reported to make the important decisions alone, but in one third of the widows' marriages the husband is said to have made the important decisions.

A similar pattern of viewing the absent husbands' contributions to the marriage in more favorable terms than do the wives of living husbands appears in answers to questions about the performance of family tasks. When asked who repaired things around the house, who mowed the lawn, who shoveled snow, and who kept track of family finances, the widows were consistently more apt than the survivors' wives to say that their husbands did these things. For all but one of these activities the proportion of the widows who cited "husband primarily" as the person who usually did these tasks was also higher than among the other miners' wives. It may be that the widows are more apt to refer to the husbands' performance of these tasks because, now that their husbands are no longer with them and the full responsibility has fallen upon them, the performances of these tasks seems especially burdensome.

The use of the comparison samples to establish probable "normal" rates for performance of the tasks by either spouse permits us to estimate how much the widows are shaping their recollections of the marriage in ways that cast the husband in a favorable light. For example, 32 percent of the widows reported that their husbands kept track of family finances, and yet in the other samples the comparable proportion is less than half of that. With respect to home repair, lawn mowing, and snow shoveling, the differences are not as large, particularly the differences between the widows and the other miners' wives. Generally widows reveal a greater role for their missing husbands than is reported in the marriages of women in the comparison samples. We would argue that the difference between the rates in the other two samples and those reported by the widows reflect the favorable bias operating to make the former marriage appear better than it was. The bias appears in a dramatic fashion with respect to reports about who did the grocery shopping. Among the widows almost half (47 percent) reported that they and their husbands did the shopping together, while in the comparison samples the rates are 24 percent and 31 percent.

This idealization of the past does not appear in every role. With respect to child-rearing duties, reports that the husband and wife perform such duties together are as common among the survivors' wives as among the widows. In the tasks traditionally done by the wife such as getting the husband's breakfast on workdays, straightening up the living room and doing evening dishes, the intersample differences are small, although they are in the direction that we would expect, given the idealization process. The widows are more slightly apt than other wives to report that they got up and fixed their husband's breakfast on workdays, are more apt to report that the wife was usually the one to straighten up the house, and are slightly less apt to report that they did the evening dishes alone.

The idealization of the missing husband is most striking in the contrast between the survivors' wives and the widows. In the recollection of family solidarity, of husbands performing the traditional family male roles, and of family togetherness in those roles traditionally shared, it appears that the marriages of the widows were happier and more solid than are the marriages of the survivors' wives. Generally but not always, the widows' marriages are also "better" than those of the other miners' wives, although in a few cases no differences appear. The average widow's marriage was better than the average marriage appeared to the people still married. At least that is how it is remembered.

References

Lopata, Helena Znaniecki. 1973. *Widowhood in an American City*. Cambridge, Mass.: Schenkman.
U.S. Bureau of the Census. 1973. *Statistical Abstract of the United States: 1973*. (94th ed.). Washington, D.C.: U.S. Government Printing Office.

3

After the Fire: Blame, Reactions, and Community Tensions

Industrial accidents, unlike natural disasters, typically lend themselves to interpretations where blame may be assigned. Recriminations may follow floods, tornados, or earthquakes because adequate safety precautions were not taken to protect the community from such "acts of God," but the event itself is usually defined as something beyond human control. An industrial fire, on the other hand, is more directly attributable to the acts of people, and much more accusation and assignment of blame might be anticipated. Conditions that produce any disaster can be blamed in some way on human error. Blame is generally put upon community authorities rather than actual perpetrators (Veltfort and Lee 1957:197-207).

Communities that experience disasters usually respond with high levels of social support, and feelings of closeness and common identity are heightened. Later the "postdisaster utopia" disappears, the unusual cohesiveness fostered by the common threat dissolves, and normal antagonisms and animosities resurface. These may be intensified by repercussions of the disaster, particularly when it may be defined as in some way caused or at least not prevented by someone's action or inaction. Sympathy with the victims may also wane, perhaps because they are no longer seen as worthy of the help afforded them. Victims may be seen as greedy or ungrateful for help received, or perhaps community members simply tire of being altruistic.

Barton (1969:301-308) discusses such processes as part of the "termination of the therapeutic social system" that invariably follows a disaster. Organizations involved in distributing relief may become objects of hostility, and often there are charges of favoritism, incompetence, and discrimination. Bates (1963:62) adds that persons who receive the most aid or experience the greatest loss and suffering are singled out and used as reference points in assessing whether one has received just treatment. Satisfaction with the treatment received depends on which of the many possible reference points is selected.

The emergence and collapse of the utopian mood that follows community response to disaster has also been described by Taylor, Zurcher, and Key (1970:160-173) who described community response to the tornado that ravaged Topeka, Kansas in 1966. Factors disruptive to the utopian mood noted by these authors include disagreements about appropriate programs for recovery, factionalism among different groups, and the emergence of the "unworthy victim." In their words,

The utopian mood is far too fragile to survive. The individual becomes once again the private citizen, concerned less with the collective need than with the cultivation of his own garden.

The utopian mood thus is self-limiting. It results from shared beliefs in the nature of the problem and in the strategies for overcoming it. It also gives rise to precise definitions of specific types of action. The focus on action produces a new reality and poses new problems. Unforeseen personal and group strains emerge. The perspectives then change, and the utopian mood fades away. Thus the utopian perspective should be seen not as cause or consequence alone, but as one stage in a continuing feedback process whereby the average citizen is able to adapt to crisis. A similar process of emergence and decay seems to occur in the early stages of development of many types of collective behavior. (Taylor, Zurcher, and Key 1970:161).

Taylor and his associates say that for every heaven, there must be a hell, and for every utopia, a scapegoat. For example, one of the liabilities of the Red Cross is that it frequently becomes the target for postdisaster scapegoating, and that was the case in Topeka. There is a built-in conflict between the bureaucratic safeguards necessary in the operation of large-scale organizations like the Red Cross and the ad hoc priorities and procedures that seem appropriate in the local setting. Moreover, people bring a variety of perspectives to a social situation, and when that situation is as intense as disaster, a variety of perspectives are likely to structure the ambiguity inherent in the continually changing situation. The differing reference groups and definitions that people bring to collective action set the stage for scapegoating. The intensity of the collective action leads people to value their own perspectives highly, but of course others may be motivated by different pressures and priorities, and thus the stage is set for stereotyping:

If one kind of perspective provides a definition of good and the true, then those who fail to accord are by definition neither good nor true, they are false and unworthy. People outside the sphere of the angels can only be devils (Taylor, Zurcher, and Key 1970:163).

Drabek and Quarantelli (1967) suggest that postdisaster scapegoating may be "rational," that is, directed at someone who could be responsible for the disaster, or "irrational," focused at those who could not be responsible. In either case scapegoating may relieve (or create) tensions but does not appear to help direct postdisaster activity toward prevention of reoccurrence, in their opinion.

Blame and Scapegoating

The people of Kellogg were quick to assign blame. When asked whether it seemed to them during the week of the fire that their associates tended to blame some person or group for the fire, more than two thirds of the women said yes. The widows said that it was the Sunshine Mine Company that most often was blamed, although the U.S. Bureau of Mines, arsonists or cigarette smokers, and specific company employees were also mentioned. While between 68 and 72 percent of the women said that those around them were blaming someone for the fire, usually the company, they were apt to say that they themselves did not hold anyone responsible for the fire during that first week. Only 27 percent of the widows, 24 percent of survivors' wives, and 26 percent of the miners' wives said that they blamed anyone for the disaster initially. Those who did generally blamed the Sunshine Mine officials. Resentment and hostility during the search for the missing men, reported in chapter 1 was generally directed toward the Sunshine management; this reaction could also be interpreted as scapegoating.

One widow who blamed the Sunshine Mine said, "They knew about unsafe conditions. We [husband and I] discussed it just two weeks before the disaster." Two other critical widows commented:

> My husband said it was always bad. Someone—maybe a lot of some-ones—were to blame. Inspectors, Department of the Interior, the company and all—maybe the union too. They knew how bad it was.

> The Bureau of Mines were bought off. If they say too much, they're afraid of their jobs. The safety engineer has no more background than I have. If a woman ran a house the way they ran that mine, it would be something.

Women who said that they did not hold anybody responsible for the fire explained that there was not enough proof to blame anyone or that during the week of the fire they could not concentrate on who to blame.

A final question about blame referred to the women's feelings at the time of the interview and read, "Now that the various hearings have been held by the Department of the Interior, the state Department of Mines, the union, and the company as to the cause of the fire, have you changed your opinion as to who was responsible for the fire?" Only a small proportion (26 percent of the widows, 18 percent of the survivors' wives, and 14 percent of the other miners' wives) said that the six months of hearings had changed their minds about who was responsible for the fire.

When asked who they currently felt should be held responsible, the most common answer for every group was "no one in particular." The predominant feeling was that the fire had "just happened." Among those who did feel that somebody was still to blame, the Sunshine Company remained the primary culprit, with 28 percent of the other miners' wives blaming the company. The most noticeable difference between the womens' responses at the time of the interview and those they reported both for themselves and for their associates at the time of the fire was that blame for safety inspectors or the Bureau of Mines had increased. In fact, the widows differed from the other two groups in this regard. Nineteen percent of them blamed either the safety inspectors or the Bureau of Mines, compared to 7 percent of the other miners' wives and only one (2 percent) of the survivors' wives. The change in widows' attitudes probably reflects the official findings of the U.S. Bureau of Mines, whose report attributed the disaster to "pedestrian" company safety practices and "obviously deficient" federal safety regulations (Franklin 1973:14).

One form of rational scapegoating evident among our respondents was the filing of lawsuits that attempted to fix blame on the Sunshine Company or the mine inspectors. Lawsuits against the state inspector of mines were anticipated by 26 widows six months after the fire. Those who anticipated suing did so for the following reasons: (1) "The mine inspector was at fault" (nine widows); (2) "Thinking of the future," presumably the economic future (four widows); (3) "Nothing to lose by it" (four widows); (4) A feeling that better safety standards might result (three widows). Others did not reply or did not give a reason for being involved in a suit (six widows).[1]

Focus on the culpability of the mine inspector was an issue in less than half of the anticipated suits, and our own expectation that the mine inspector would be a scapegoat did not materialize. In the free response question on who the subjects currently hold responsible, only three widows noted that "safety inspectors" were to blame.

Said one who was suing, "I'm not out to get even, but my husband would want me to be well taken care of. They took my husband's life because of neglect. This money is needed to provide for me." Another said, "I was asked to [sue]. If I'm entitled, I might as well get it." The interviewer noted that this woman was very worried about medical bills because without her husband she no longer had the medical insurance that had been one of his occupational benefits. Some of the widows were confused by the legal maneuvers: One appeared not to know for sure in what she was involved, stating, "I signed my name to something that an attorney from Los Angeles wanted. She said we're all going to do it."

The nonsuers were also sympathetic to those widows who would sue. One said, "I don't think the suit is against the mine inspector. I have mixed feelings because I don't hold the mine inspector responsible. If money is gained from such a suit, my children are entitled to it." Another said, "Bills are the same without my husband. They had a form at union headquarters saying if we got anything [from a suit], we would have to pay back all the workmen's compensation we've received."

Social conflict over relief and reconstruction is common in communities affected by disaster. The operation of relief agencies may change the relative positions of the rich and poor and create resentment. Barton (1969:309-310) notes that the distribution of aid according to level of need rather than amount of loss may create situations where the poor end up better off than they ever were. Thus aid distributed according to equalitarian norms may induce feelings of relative deprivation among people of the upper and middle classes for whom restoration frequently means restoration to the conditions of inequality which existed prior to the disaster rather than to the conditions of relative equality which existed immediately after the disaster. Well-meaning relief efforts and altruistic programs may, therefore, create conflict, bitterness, and complaint, as well as sharpen divisions within the community. We did not find rescuers being blamed in this disaster.

Two men lived in the Sunshine Mine for a week before the rescuers found them, and they were the only survivors. We asked our subjects how they felt about the fact that survivors were found. While most respondents felt that finding survivors was "wonderful" or they were "happy for those families," a minority expressed resentment, which we interpret as irrational scapegoating. Twelve percent of the widows, 6 percent of the survivors' wives, and 4 percent of the other miners' wives group suggested that "especially those two" were not people that should have been saved because they were "lazy" or had "hidden out." Hostility toward the survivors was exemplified by a widow who said, "I didn't think it was fair. Ex-cons and drug addicts. My husband was going to fire one. They were back in some hole sleeping is why they got out. The Sunshine didn't gain a thing by finding them." Another said, "They were back in a hole before the fire began, goofing off."

In contrast were the attitudes shown by a widow who was waiting at the mine site when she got the news, saying, "We cried. We were so happy we jumped up and down." Another said, "I prayed for them. It was the most wonderful thing that ever happened." Some found the rescue of the two a cause for renewed hope: "I doubted anyone would make it. I was happy and thought they'd find others. I'm thankful for the two—I sure didn't begrudge them." Another said, "The Lord had a purpose in saving those two."

Some who did not blame the survivors were nonetheless resentful. One woman admitted, "I was resentful because my husband wasn't one of them." Another said, "When they found them, they told us they were pumping air down there. We just knew my husband would be alive."

Open hostility to the press, reported in a previous chapter, may also reflect irrational scapegoating. Neither the press nor the two survivors could have been responsible for the fire, but hostility toward them might have been a mechanism used by some women for relieving tensions.

Memorial Fund and Community Tensions

Initially several memorial funds were established in the Coeur d'Alene mining district for the benefit of families of the victims of the fire. First reactions to these funds were overwhelmingly supportive. Most of the women said they had "thought it was wonderful." After the search for the missing men ended, however, the funds were consolidated in the Miners' Memorial Educational Fund to provide college scholarships for the victims' children. This fund was less well received, particularly by widows who were directly affected. Sixteen of the 44 widows thought the idea was a good one, provided funds were channeled correctly; an equal number were dissatisfied. The dissatisfied widows felt the fund should not concentrate only on children's education but instead should include the whole family and have provision for immediate needs. For example, a widow with very young children felt that educational needs for her family were far in the future and that other needs were much more pressing. Other widows felt deprived because their children were not planning to go to college. One said, "My son wants to be a truck driver. Shouldn't there be help for him too?"

There were no widows on the board that administers the fund, and the chairman of the fund was and still is a mining official from the area. Perhaps the dissatisfaction on the part of some widows could have been eliminated by their more direct participation.

For all three groups of women the proportion expressing approval and support for the Miners' Memorial Educational Fund at the time of the interview was lower than the proportion who said they felt good about the various memorial funds as initially established. Eighty percent of the widows and 84 percent of both the survivors' wives and the other miners' wives expressed approval when asked, "How did you feel about the funds at the time?" When asked how they now felt about the Miners' Memorial Educational Fund, the consolidation of the funds established earlier, responses were much more negative: Thirty-six percent of the widows, 40 percent of the survivors' wives, and 59 percent of the other miners' wives gave an unqualified positive response. The widows' and survivors' wives were much more likely to see the consolidated fund as a "big fraud," or "channeled to the wrong place." Proportions of the three groups giving clearly negative definitions, in contrast to expressions of mixed feelings, were 36 percent, 38 percent, and 23 percent, respectively.

The sharp contrast between the agreement among the three groups in reactions to the initial funds and the essentially negative feelings of widows' and survivors' wives, but not other miners' wives, about the consolidated educational fund may reflect differences in perceptions about the extent of loss and "rightful recompense" following loss. It may also reflect a lack of careful analysis by the other miners' wives about the relative benefits and disadvantages of the consolidated fund. For the survivors and widows, however, the contrast between the benefits of the consolidated fund and "what might have been" are much more striking, and they are bitter about the perceived loss of benefit.

In a negative and inaccurate reaction to the fund, one widow said, "Always before the Sunshine had had $300 scholarships for *all* of their miners and children going to college. Now my child can only get a total of $300 for scholarship. The Sunshine discontinued their fund." Another woman complained at great length about the fund; she and other widows had talked about it a lot and resented that the fund was college oriented: "It isn't right; women without children don't get nothing."

Another widow who was one course short of high school graduation and wanted to go to college wanted support for her own education, saying, "People contributed under the idea that the funds were for *all* of the *family*." There were also complaints about the administration of the fund. A widow remarked, "Probably won't be long before . . . [administrator of fund] will put a new roof on the Old Mission [a national historical monument in the area]." Other comments by widows expressing dissatisfaction or perceived injustice:

> I got a letter from the Sunshine for future children and was told the fund was only for those who needed help and for future men who are killed even in other mines. When people gave money it was to be for Sunshine miners' children. They [board of fund] won't tell—I don't know how it's to be determined who gets the fund.

> I'm frightened that the kids will never get it. I've already gotten a letter saying that only *deserving* children will get money from the fund.

> The fund is a big phony. It wasn't done in a democratic manner. The two survivors got $1000 and paid education and they can still earn. Where is my $1000 and money for education? I lost my husband's earning power. My children aren't that intelligent and won't get funds. I went to my lawyer about things, but they won't fight the bigwigs.[2]

Assessments of Federal and State Response

The governor of Idaho attempted to have the Coeur d'Alene Mining District declared a national disaster area during the week of search. This request was turned down despite the fact that President Nixon had wired the community expressing concern and support. Seventy-three percent of the widows said they disagreed with the federal government's negative decision, as compared to 54 percent of the survivors' wives and 48 percent of the other miners' wives. The women most directly affected were the ones who were most upset with the federal decision.

One widow commented:

> It's ridiculous for Nixon to offer us help and then turn us down. It was a disaster to us. Considering the population, it affected so many here. All the support came from the local people. The federal government should have helped more.

Another said:

> If any other tragedy killed 91 people—or in a metropolitan area—it would
> have been more political, and it would have been a disaster. They think
> we're peons. The president never said anything.

Another critic said, "They'd have helped if we had lost material things—
just husbands didn't matter them."

That a woman's perceptions of the intensity and nature of the disaster
were influenced by its effect upon her own role relationships is apparent in
the women's comments about whether they agreed with the federal decision
not to declare the community a disaster area. Only 18 percent of the widows
responded that they felt the community had everything it needed to cope
with the disaster or that it did not meet the federal specifications for designa-
tion as a disaster area. Corresponding proportions of survivors' and other
miners' wives were 36 percent and 44 percent. The greater the personal loss,
or the closer the respondents were to direct personal loss, then the less apt
they were to see local resources as adequate or to cite bureaucratic regulations as a justifiable reason for defining the disaster as local in scope. Stated
differently, the greater the proximity to personal loss, the greater the
tendency to define the disaster in extralocal terms. Comments from widows
who agreed with the federal decision may be useful to illustrate the minority
point of view:[3] "We weren't really a disaster like a flood or the whole town
burning down," and, "As experts they knew what they were doing. Didn't
lose our homes and property. We had food and all we needed except
husbands."

Assessments of Mining as an Occupation

It seemed likely that some of the negative feelings created by the disaster
would be directed at mining as an occupation. After all, had the victims not
been miners, they would not have been in hazard in the first place. As expected, widows were more apt to define mining negatively or to stress that
they didn't like their men doing it than were the other respondents. (Proportions describing mining as hazardous, needing to be made safer, or as an
undesirable occupation were 41 percent, 20 percent, and 24 percent, respectively.) Rather than defining mining as a gloomy and hazardous occupation
as did Lucas's (1969) subjects in a coal-mining community, our respondents
who were not widowed by the Sunshine fire seemed to hold the view of the
disaster as idiosyncratic and unlikely to recur. In answer to the question,
"What is your opinion of mining as an occupation?", we obtained the
distribution of responses shown in table 3-1.

Table 3-1
Perceptions of Mining as an Occupation
(percent)

Perceptions of Mining	Widows	Survivors' Wives	Other Miners' Wives
It's up to the men	32	29	24
Don't like it	22	12	7
Someone has to do it	16	10	4
Very hazardous	16	7	16
No more hazardous than any other	11	32	41
Other	3	10	8
Total	100	100	100
(*N*)	(37)	(41)	(114)

The most common response for widows shows "It's up to the men," whereas "no more hazardous than any other" turned up most frequently for the other two groups. Widows, dramatically and directly affected by the Sunshine disaster, were more negative. The results in table 3-1 would have occurred by chance less than five times in a thousand.

"It's up to the man," the most common widow's response, was second for both the survivors (29 percent) and the other miners' wives (24 percent). This response sugggests an attitude of resignation, coupled with a strict division of labor by sex. A man's role is to make a living, and these women saw the choice of how that would be accomplished as up to the person doing the work. Fewer of these wives were in the labor force themselves than was the national average for married women in 1972, and their husbands made more money in 1971 than many other men of similar education. One surviving wife said she had "wanted my husband to quit mining for a long time, but without experience and education, he can do nothing else. The job pays enough to support our family on this, and with poor education, he couldn't get anything else." One widow who expressed this view said, "It's a man's life, and he has to choose." Another said, "It's a job, and especially if a man enjoyed it [as her husband did], he should do it." A third said, "It's a job. My husband loved the work. Besides, it keeps the smelter and the zinc plant going." Someone else felt, "Mining is a necessary occupation, and someone has to do it." Another widow said, "Six feet under is deep enough for me. It's all right if a man likes it—if a few laws were passed and adequately enforced."

Survivors' wives and other miners' wives were most likely to define mining as "no more hazardous than any other job." Comments accompanying this response were, "It's like anything else. It's no more dangerous than something else," and "There's danger any place you work. My husband is very careful." Often the women referred to the danger in other types of work: "Mining is just as good as anything else. It's a job," said one, and another concluded, "It's as safe as another labor job; it all depends upon the man."

Despite the recent disaster, even a few of the widows defined mining as no more hazardous than another job. Note, for example, these comments by the recently bereaved:

> I grew up with mining—my father was a miner for 34 years. It is no more dangerous than anything else. I'd like to see my boys do something else, but I wouldn't stand in their way.

> It's just as safe underground. It's a job, and especially if a man enjoyed it [he should do it]. He loved his mining.

> It's no more dangerous than going down the freeway.

> If you're going to get it, you'll get it anyway. He figured he was safe.

> I was never worried. He like his work.

The second most common response of widows was, "I don't like it" (22 percent). "I hope none of my family works at the mine," said one widow. Another noted that her son had mined for one year, and, "He will never go back, and I am glad of it." "I'd never want my son to mine because he lost his father," said a third widow. Another felt she would worry if she would ever remarry a miner. A fifth said, "I wouldn't want to see anyone go into mining. My husband was only [planning to be] a miner to get enough money for his education. I'd never want anyone to work in a mine, unless, like my father-in-law, that's all he knows."

In contrast, the "I don't like it" attitude was stated by only 12 percent of the survivors' wives and 7 percent of the wives of other miners. Since they were interviewed only six months after the Sunshine disaster, we anticipated a higher antipathy toward mining, with overtones of attitudes such as "There, but for the grace of God, go I." That expectation was not borne out. In fact, we had some trouble getting the other miners' wives to cooperate in the study because many said, "Why talk to me? I wasn't involved in the Sunshine disaster." Being involved evidently meant, "I didn't lose a husband or son." Moreover, the responses of the survivors' wives clearly resembled those of the other miners' wives' more than the widows'.

Indicative of the "someone has to do it" orientation are the following statements by widows:

> Mining is a necessary occupation, and someone has to do it.

> I would do nothing to stop my son from going into mining.

Someone has to do it. All occupations have hazards.

My husband was proud of his work, and he loved mining. It's a shame so many men had to be lost before they tightened up on safety precautions.

The attitude of resignation, "someone has to," was much less common among the survivors' wives and other miners' wives, with 10 and 4 percent, respectively, giving the answer.

The idea that mining is "very hazardous" was expressed by 16 percent of widows, 7 percent of survivors' wives, and 16 percent of the other wives. It was the least common response (in sixth place) for survivors' wives, and third for other miners' wives. One widow said, "I hope they close 'em all down, especially the Sunshine. It's worse [now] than it ever was." Another said, "Mining is more hazardous than other jobs, because there are a lot of accidents."

"Mining is hazardous and necessary," said a widow, and further, "The Bureau of Mines is not worth 2 cents in Chinese money."

A survivor's wife who felt mining was hazardous said, "It's one of the worst possible jobs anyone can hold. I don't want my sons underground. I wish my husband would quit going underground." Other comments by survivors' wives in the same vein:

It's necessary for some, but I'm glad he's out of it.

I was much happier when my husband worked top side. I would never do it.

It's work. Dangerous. You look at things differently when you're short of money.

Women whose husbands were still working in other mines in the Coeur d'Alene area had similar comments about the hazards of mining:

My husband and dad have made a good living with mining. It's dangerous, [but] something can happen walking across the street. . . .

I don't like it. I'm always afraid something bad will happen.

I feel the mine is just as safe an occupation as the men themselves make it. If they do a slip-shod job, it will be unsafe.

In addition to the results reported in table 3-1, 16 percent of the 44 widows had "no opinion" about mining as an occupation, as did nearly one fourth of the survivors' wives and 11 percent of the other miners' wives. It seems probable that the "up to the man" idea also characterized those wives with "no opinion."

Despite the hazards, many miners find the work all right. They believe the pay is good, and their generally favorable attitudes are reflected in their wives' attitudes.

Attitudes toward mining as an occupation were among the themes picked up by the newspeople at the time of the disaster, and some of their insights are worth noting. One reporter noted that "Mining is a family thing here. Sons follow fathers, brothers follow brothers" (Roberts 1972). When he tried to get answers to the question of why men continue working in the hard and dangerous occupation, however, he frequently heard that there was nothing else to do. Also emphasized though was the special nature of mining and how it "gets in your blood." A miner's wife told the reporter:

> Twenty years ago . . . my father left the mines because his brother-in-law got killed. But he was so unhappy he went back in. He told my mom that he didn't realize how much he would miss it. He said they don't even talk the same language above ground (Roberts 1972).

That positive attitude is repeated in the comments of many miners. The husband of the woman quoted above summarized some of the factors that kept him there, despite the danger and the difficult working conditions:

> It's a fascinating thing. . . . Boring ahead and looking for metal. And the relations between the men are very special. You get to be like one big family; you know everybody. Working underground you know 400 or 500 different families. You work together and you play together—something gets in your blood (Roberts 1972).

In stark contrast stands one of our subjects, a widow, who indicts mining as a way of life:

> I wouldn't want to see anyone going into the mining. My husband was only a miner to get enough money for his education. I never want anyone to work in a mine, unless, like my father-in-law, that's all he knows. No miner is healthy.

Notes

1. According to information received in 1977 from a Boise attorney, lawsuits were of two types: (1) victims suing the mine and other companies such as the one making respirators as well as federal and state officials, and (2) companies involved in countersuits. The first round in court, in 1978-1979, resulted in some out-of-court settlements as well as moving litigation against officials to U.S. District Court (see epilogue). Cash settlements by some of these out-of-court resolutions of suits have presumably been made to widows and other survivors (parents, children, or other family members).

2. According to formation in personal communication by H.F. Magnuson, Wallace, Idaho, to C. Harvey, August 9, 1977, "any dependent child of one of the deceased miners after they reach seventeen years of age can receive a scholarship from our Fund by merely filling out a short application . . . along with a letter from a college, university, or other training school showing that such person has been accepted for admission." As of April 30, 1977, 30 people had received money from the fund, in amounts from $300 to $4,823 per person, to attend colleges, universities, trade and technical schools, and one other school. At least 23 families of victims were represented, with two families having 3 persons as recipients. (It would be possible that more families are represented; for example, first cousins often have the same family name, *or* same family names are not relatives as in *Johnson.*)

3. The Sunshine Mine Fire was *not* declared a Federal Disaster; the Silver Valley Flood (Coeur d'Alene River Valley Flood) *was* declared a Federal Disaster in 1974. (See Epilogue.) We interpret this to mean that life-lost disasters are not disasters, but property-lost disasters are, at least in two Idaho cases, 1972 and 1974.

References

Barton, Allen H. 1969. *Communities in Disaster: A Sociological Analysis of Collective Stress Situations.* New York: Doubleday.

Bates, F.L. 1963. (C.W. Fogleman; V.J. Parenton, R.H. Pittman, and G.S. Tracy) "The Social and Psychological Consequences of a Natural Disaster: A Longitudinal Study of Hurricane Audrey." *Disaster Study Number 18*, Washington, D.C.: National Academy of Sciences—National Research Council.

Drabek, Thomas, and Quarentelli, E.L. 1967. "Scapegoats, Villians and Disaster." *Transaction* 4 (March):12-17.

Franklin, Ben A. 1973. "Safety Held Lax in 91 Mine Deaths." *New York Times*, February 14, p. 14.

Lucas, Rex A. 1969. *Men in Crisis: A Study of a Mine Disaster.* New York: Basic Books.

Roberts, Steven V. 1972. "Idaho's 'Hard Rock' Miners: 'They Work Hard, Play Hard and Don't Save a Dime, but They Enjoy Life.'" *New York Times* (May 7):34.

Taylor, James B., Zurcher, Louis A., and Key, William H. 1970. *Tornado.* Seattle: University of Washington Press.

Veltfort, Helene Rank, and Lee, George E. 1957. "The Coconut Grove Fire: A Study in Scapegoating." In *Collective Behavior*, ed. Ralph H. Turner and Lewis M. Killian, pp. 197-207. Englewood Cliffs, N.J.: Prentice-Hall.

4 Adjustments in the Social Network

There are two major components in the literature on widowhood. First are the studies of adjustment done by identifying newly bereaved persons and interviewing them one or more times in the succeeding months to assess their reactions and adjustment to the new status, and second are studies of widowed persons located as part of general population surveys. Most of those in the former category have focused primarily on dimensions of psychological and physical well-being. Examples of the psychological adjustment studies of the newly widowed include Clayton (1973, 1974), Clayton et al. (1972, 1973), Parkes and Brown (1972), Bornstein et al. (1973), Briscoe and Smith (1975), and Carey (1977).

Some of the surveys of widows of the second type, who are part of general population surveys include measures of attitudes (Gubrium 1974; Harvey and Bahr 1974). These are much more apt than the studies of the newly bereaved to pay attention to differences between the widowed and others in extent of social affiliation and participation. For example, Bock and Webber (1972) consider ties to kin and organizational membership of widows as factors mitigating the social isolation of widows; Berardo (1967) contrasts the family friendship and formal organizational participation of the widowed with the married; Lopata (1973) devotes a substantial part of her book to a consideration of the kinship roles, friendship ties, and community involvement patterns of Chicago widows; Harvey and Bahr (1974) report the voluntary affiliation rates of widows in five countries; and Atchley (1975) compares the social and voluntary affiliation rates of widows in five countries; and Atchley (1975) compares the social participation of married and widowed retired persons. There is also literature urging greater attention to the social ties of widows, from both scientific and social-work perspectives (Lopata, 1972; Walker, MacBride, and Vachon 1977; McCourt et al. 1976).

Much less common are studies that bridge these two streams of research about widowhood and examine changes in the social relationships of the newly widowed, although there is some relevant autobiographical and journalistic literature (Caine 1974; Lewis 1975). This chapter assesses the social relationships of women bereaved in the 1972 Sunshine Mine fire in Kellogg, Idaho. Specifically, we shall pay attention to changes in relationships with relatives, friends, and community organizations.

Modes of Adjustment to Widowhood

The most notable recent work on the social adjustment of the newly widowed was done by Glick, Weiss, and Parkes (1974:231-259) who analyzed data from multiple interviews with persons aged forty-five and under widowed in the Boston area in 1965-1966. They developed a typology of "patterns of recovery" based largely on the changes in widowed persons' social relationships following widowhood. They designate five "alternate directions in life organization": (1) movement toward remarriage; (2) adoption of the widow role and relative independence from close relationships with others; (3) adoption of the widow role and life organization about a nonmarital relationship with men; (4) adoption of the widow role and establishment of a life pattern around relationships to kin; and (5) failure to recover as indicated by chaotic life organization. They also group these five into three more inclusive categories, namely, movement toward remarriage, movement in other directions toward reorganization, and failure to move toward reorganization. These three categories parallel the three options for American widows outlined by Lopata as regaining past social relations, engaging in new social roles, or becoming isolated (Lopata 1970:55).

In our view these three options may be clarified by referring to them in the terminology of affiliation theory as continuity, replacement, and withdrawal. "Continuity" refers to those situations where the loss of a husband does not affect a woman's attitudes and activities very much. This type of adjustment (or lack of adjustment) may characterize women whose lives were largely independent of their husbands prior to their deaths, as in cases where separate residences are maintained or where the widow's financial situation and social life remains fairly constant despite the bereavement. It also applies to widows who resume the same friendship and organizational ties they maintained before widowhood, after a period of grief and personal adjustment.

A second mode of adjustment is the "replacement" approach, in which loss of a husband's companionship and social support is made up by the formation of new ties of kinship, friendship, or community responsibility. The most obvious example of total replacement is remarriage, but it can take many forms and may be partial or complete. Adjustment by replacement is illustrated in a widow's immersion in employment, activation of kinship ties, increasing devotion to family and children, or greater activity in community organizations.

A third type of adjustment is withdrawal-disaffiliation. We use the pair of terms to describe it because this type of adjustment may not be entirely or even largely a matter of voluntary choice by the widow, yet the term "withdrawal," by itself, suggests that it is. It occurs because social ties that existed at the time of widowhood are weakened or lost but not replaced by other ties. Withdrawal-disaffiliation can be viewed as a general contraction of the social world of the widow, a turning inward. Presumably this mode is more common among persons widowed in old age for whom replacement may be more difficult than for younger persons.

The study of adjustment to widowhood is complicated by the fact that women may progress through all three types. One may move from continuity to withdrawal, and then begin a personal program of replacement. An example would be a widow who maintains her old friendship ties for a time and then gradually finds them unsatisfactory because they involve other couples. Next she stops doing things with these couples and is a loner for a time, and then she finds a new set of friends more compatible with her present interests and situation. Another widow might pass through the same three types of adjustment in a different order, as though the types were stages in an evolutionary process. Of course, the sequence of changes in social network that follows widowhood takes more than six months, and because the interviews took place six months after the fire, we will present information about only the first part of the process now. (Chapter 8 contains more information about adjustment to widowhood.)

The major objective of this chapter is to determine to what extent continuity, replacement, or withdrawal are apparent in the social relationships of the newly widowed. Our method of answering it will be to examine the social contacts of the widowed as contrasted with those of comparison samples of women in the same community having similar characteristics. If our main proposition were stated in null terms, it would be that the newly widowed do not differ significantly from the nonwidowed in their contacts with friends and relatives or in their organizational ties.

Contacts with Friends and Relatives

Family Relationships

There are two questions in the interview schedule directly relevant to interaction with relatives. One asked whether the woman had any close relatives in the Kellogg area, and identified these as parents, brothers, sisters, aunts, or uncles. There was also a question about current contact with relatives, with specific probes for visiting, telephoning, and writing letters. Somewhat less relevant to the question of adjustment to widowhood were questions about immediate actions during the fire, which included behaviors toward family members as possible options. These questions included the following: "Did you alert anyone such as other miners' wives, neighbors, or family members about the possibility of trouble at the mine?";

"Who did you feel you could lean on most for comfort and reassurance during the fire?"; and "Who was the most responsive to your emotional needs during the week of the disaster?"

Even before the fire the women to be widowed in the Sunshine disaster were somewhat less likely than other women in the area to have the support of close relatives living nearby. Fifty-one percent of the widows said they had close relatives in the surrounding area, compared to 58 percent of the survivors' wives and 63 percent of the other miners' wives. When we generalize about frequency of contact with kin and the possibilities of social and emotional support from relatives, it must be recognized that for half the widows there were no close relatives immediately available.

The widows' lower level of involvement with kin was apparent in their responses to news of trouble at the mine. Twenty-seven percent said that they alerted in-laws or members of their immediate family, a comparatively low proportion when we recognize that among the other miners' wives—women not directly threatened by the trouble—32 percent contacted in-laws or immediate family, as did 36 percent of the survivors' wives. The relative lack of availability of kin was reflected in the widows' communication patterns during the disaster.

The relative deprivation of the widows with respect to support from kin is further illustrated in the number of them who included "immediate family" in their answer to the question about whom they felt they could "lean on the most for comfort and reassurance during the fire." In contrast to the stark, seemingly hopeless situation of the widows, the survivors' wives and the other miners' wives knew that their husbands were safe—at least nearly all the survivors' wives knew by the end of the first day—and yet they reported some need for "comfort and reassurance" during the week. Seventy-seven percent of the other miners' wives and 68 percent of the survivors' wives said they received support and reassurance from close relatives. In contrast, only 56 percent of the widows said that they could lean on immediate family for such support. The same general pattern appeared in answer to the question, "Who was the most responsive to your emotional needs. . .?" For widows, 60 percent said, "immediate family," compared to 69 percent of survivors' wives and 77 percent of other wives.

Not only was positive support from relatives less frequently available to widows but also some of them had negative feelings about relatives who were available. The fact that such definitions were slightly more common among the widows than among other women reflects the increasing strain widows experienced as the week progressed; furthermore, the widows were more apt to be the objects of sympathy or to face relatives in an unfamiliar situation. Asked if they felt uncomfortable around some people during the week of the search, 39 percent of the widows (30 percent of the survivors' wives and 29 percent of the other miners' wives) said yes, and almost half of these identified relatives as persons who made them feel uncomfortable. (Five of the 17 widows who agreed that someone made them uncomfortable identified relatives explicitly, and two others included relatives in the general response "everyone.")

Although there was no item that dealt specifically with changes in kin relationships, some indications of present interaction levels were obtained. Asked about visits and phone calls to relatives during the previous week, about three-fourths of the widows reported at least one visit and at least one telephone call. These rates of contact were slightly higher than for survivors' wives (68 percent reported a visit and 64 percent had at least one call) and slightly lower than the rates of kin contact reported by other miners' wives (83 percent and 81 percent).

The fact that the widows' currently interacted with kin at about the same level as the other groups is notable. Widows had fewer kin available in the area, and they had consistently lower levels of involvement with relatives prior to and during the fire. Apparently a response to widowhood among these women was a reestablishment and strengthening of ties to relatives so that their present interaction with kin is on a par with that of the other two samples. The increase in kinship solidarity is not large—widows' rates of visiting and telephoning kin six months after the fire were not unusually high, merely "normal" in terms of the kinship interaction of other women in the community—but achievement of normality represents a modest increase in kinship interaction for the widows, an increase more notable because they were slightly less likely than women in the other groups to have close relatives living nearby.

The finding that adjustment to widowhood may involve increased solidarity with kin is corroborated in the report of the first year of bereavement by Glick, Weiss, and Parkes (1974:234). Among the 47 widows whose lifeways were distributed by Glick and his associates among five distinctive patterns of adjustment, five (11 percent) fit the "life pattern around relationships with kin." In contrast 14 were in the category "movement toward remarriage," and 17 in the "independent of close relationships with other adults." There were 5 whose lives were organized around a nonmarital relationship with a man and 6 who were considered to have a chaotic life organization (Glick, Weiss, and Parkes, 1974:232-254).

The emphasis of Glick and his colleagues on the importance of relatives in adjustment to widowhood needs to be tempered by recognizing that relatives are also important to the nonwidowed. While the widows were more apt to single out family members than anyone else when asked who had been most helpful to them in their bereavement, it is likely that if nonwidows were asked who had been most helpful in some other respect, at least as many would mention relatives. As our comparative statistics indicate, the Sunshine Mine widows were most apt to single out "immediate family'' as most helpful and responsive, and yet the levels of reported support and responsiveness among kin were no higher for the Kellogg widows than for the nonwidowed samples. It is not that widowhood creates ties to kin where none existed before but rather that relatives are important in coping with most family crises.

Friendship

Answers to a series of questions about friendship ties to other women in the community before the fire establish that the friendship networks of women in the three samples were fairly similar. The questions were designed to reflect increasing levels of intensity of friendship, with the first one referring to a generalized attitude of friendliness, "Did you consider yourself to be friendly with women in the community before the fire?" That was followed by a report of joint activity, "Did you participate in social activities. . . ?", and then there was a question about whether the respondent had had a truly close friend, a confidant: "Some people have close friends to whom they can confide their worries, hopes, dreams, and problems. Did you have close friends of this type . . . ?" Each of these questions was asked twice, once as applied to women who were the wives of miners and once for women who were wives of men in other occupations.

Almost all the women (90 percent or more in every sample) said that they were friendly with other women in the community, and the reported levels of social participation and close friendship with wives whose husbands were not miners were the same (social participation, 72 percent, 62 percent, and 72 percent, respectively, and having a close friend, 70 percent, 76 percent, and 73 percent). Widows were slightly less likely to report social particpiation and close friendship with wives of miners than were women in the other samples. Half the widows said they socialized with wives of miners, compared to 56 percent of the survivors' wives and 72 percent of the other miners' wives, and the same differential appeared for the question on close friends who were miners' wives (49 percent, versus 60 and 68 percent, respectively). Despite this tendency for slightly less friendship involvement with miners' wives, the widows were as involved in friendship networks generally. The three samples of women exhibited similar levels of friendship and social participation before the fire, although there seem to have been some differences in friends' characteristics.

For measures of friendship activity at the time of the interview, there were questions on frequency of visits and telephone calls to friends, plus a question on whether the women participated in social activities offered by local churches. Another question treated changes in friendship patterns explicitly: "Since the mine disaster, has your group of friends changed?" A certain amount of change would be anticipated in any six-month period. Judging from the reports of the survivors' wives and other miners' wives, we would estimate the normal turnover in friends for this six-month period to be between 10 and 20 percent. The reported rates of change for women in both these groups was a little higher than that—28 percent and 15 percent—but in both comparison samples, the most common explanation for change in friendship networks was that some of their friends had been lost in the fire.

Change in friends among the widows was far more frequent than the expected rate noted above: almost half of them (48 percent) said their group of friends had changed since the fire. Moreover, *none* of the widows who said their friends had changed attributed the change to having lost friends in the fire. The primary reason given was not that their friends have moved or that they have been lost in the fire, but rather that they no longer saw their married friends anymore. Along with the change to status of widow had come strains, new definitions, or feelings of ''being in the way'' or ''being extra,'' which combined to weaken or dissolve the old friendships. Nine of the 21 widows who said their friendship group had changed attributed the change to the fact that they did not see their married friends anymore.

Although their friendship groups might have changed, there was no evidence that the widows suffered from lack of friends. Three fourths of the women in all three samples reported at least one visit with friends during the previous week. Thirty percent of the widows reported five or more visits during that period, compared to 10 percent of the survivors' wives and 26 percent of the other miners' wives.

Details about differences between the samples in amount of communication with friends during the week before the interview are presented in figure 4-1. There are some minor intersample differences: for visits with friends, the widows are slightly underrepresented at the low end of the scale (fewer of them report one or two visits than do the other women). They are correspondingly overrepresented at the upper end of the scale, that is, the widows are a little more likely than the other miners' wives and much more likely than the survivors' wives to report visits with friends on a daily or more-than-daily basis. The most dramatic finding apparent in figure 4-1 is the remarkable similarity in the profiles, especially the ones for visiting by telephone. Typically the range of difference among the three samples is 10 percent or less. Accordingly we conclude that in frequency of communication with friends, the widows are very similar to the other women.

It might be argued that because they are without mates, friendship ought to play a much greater role in the widows' lives. If that is so, then evidence that their rates of contact with friends were about the same as those for married women might be seen as evidence that the widows suffer relative deprivation: others have husbands *and* friends, the widows have

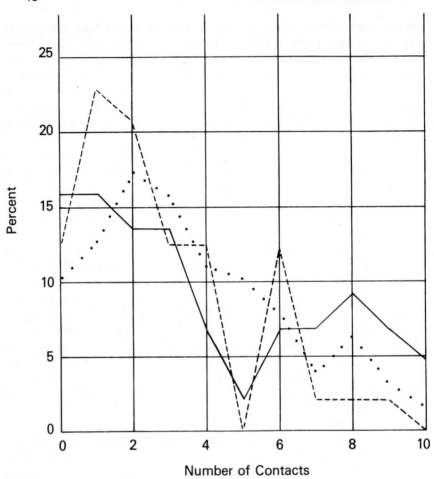

Widows
- - - -   Survivors' wives
. . . .   Other miners' wives

Figure 4-1. Number of Contacts (Telephone Calls or Personal Visits) with
Friends During Past Week.

only friends. Evaluation of this argument would require more data on the
nature and quality of friendship than we had available, but we suspect that
there might be some compensations operating in the widows' favor. It may
be that a widow's visit with a friend was a more extended event, if only
because the widow didn't have to worry about getting ready for husband's

arrival at home or adjusting things to his schedule. But these are specula-
tions; our data simply show that the widows visit and telephone friends
about as much as other women do.

These results do not yield much evidence of the "withdrawal" mode of
adpating to widowhood. Instead, there is some evidence of continuity and
even more for replacement, both with respect to friendship and kinship ties.
The widows' ties to relatives seem stronger than before, and their friendships are as frequent, although many of their former married friends seem
to have been replaced by others.

A Summary Measure of Social Contact

Some advantage may be gained by combining the data on present contact
with relatives and friends into a single measure of personal interaction with
significant others, as use of the separate indicators of interaction does not
allow us to identify those isolated women who had contacts with neither
friends nor relatives. In other words, inspection of the distribution of
women by degree of contact with relatives may tell us that between one
fourth and one third of the women in all three samples did not telephone
friends during the week preceding the interview and also that between one
fourth and one third did not visit friends during the same week. It does not,
however, tell us whether those who did not visit were the same as those who
did not call, if the noncallers all made contact by visiting, or how many
women had no contact either by telephone or by personal visit.

To remedy this defect in the use of the separate indicators of social contact, we arbitrarily defined visits and telephone calls as roughly equivalent
forms of communication and combined the scores for the various intensities
of communication with both friends and relatives into a summary scale of
social contact. Because this scale was created by summing scores for
grouped data, it is best interpreted simply as a measure of intensity of contact and is not readily interpretable into numbers of visits, except at the
lowest levels of interaction. For example a score of 1 on the summary scale
may mean one of four things. It can mean (1) one or two visits with relatives
but no visits with friends and no telephone conversations with either friends
or relatives, or (2) one or two visits with friends but no visits with relatives
and no telephone conversations with either friends or relatives, or (3) one or
two telephone conversations with friends but no telephone conversations
with relatives and no visits with friends or relatives, or (4) one or two
telephone conversations with relatives but none with friends and no personal visits with either. Of course interpreting the higher scores on the index
is much more difficult, as there are many different combinations of visits
and calls that could produce, say, a scale score of 7.

The possible range of the summary scale was 0-20, and the actual range obtained was 0-18. Despite its difficulties of literal interpretation, the summary measure of social contact does simplify matters, for it combines four separate indicators into a global measure of extent of present interaction with friends and relatives, and we may discuss a single score rather than four scores.

The distributions of scores on the summary social contact scale are presented by sample in figure 4-2. If we trace carefully the profile for the widows and compare it to the others, at least two things stand out. First, in extent of social contact, the widows are definitely on a par with the other samples. The profile for the widows is very similar to that for the other miners' wives (the average or mean summary social contact scores for the two groups are, respectively, 6.77 and 7.05, compared to 5.85 for the survivors' wives). Second, the survivors' wives are somewhat overrepresented at the lower levels of social contact (for them the modal summary score is 2, compared to 4 for the widows and both 4 and 7 for the other miners' wives). One fourth of survivors' wives have summary scores of 2 or lower, compared to only about one tenth of the widows and the other miners' wives.

The essential point is that widows definitely are not low in social contact. Of course, the reports summarized in figure 4-2 do not reflect quality or intensity of contact, merely incidence. Our simple counting of numbers of visits and telephone calls may have overlooked some important qualitative differences, but there are definitely no grounds for viewing the group of Sunshine Mine widows as socially isolated.

These findings have no necessary bearing on whether a woman *feels* lonely or not. Conceivably, the widows could have networks of social interaction as extensive as those of other women and yet feel isolated and lonely because their range of social contacts did not provide enough intense, supportive, or meaningful ties.

Let us emphasize that in all three samples there are a few isolated women. We shall explore some of the characteristics of such women in later chapters. The presence of such women, however, cannot be attributed to the fact of widowhood; most widows have as many social contacts as anyone else.

Letter Writing

Another way of being bound in social networks is through the written word. To determine if there were any differences among the samples in level of written correspondence, we asked, "In the past week how many times did you write a personal letter?" As summarized in table 4-1, the responses corroborate the general patterns of social interaction we have already noted, namely, that the widows have about the same degree of interaction as the other women. Almost half of all respondents said that they had not written

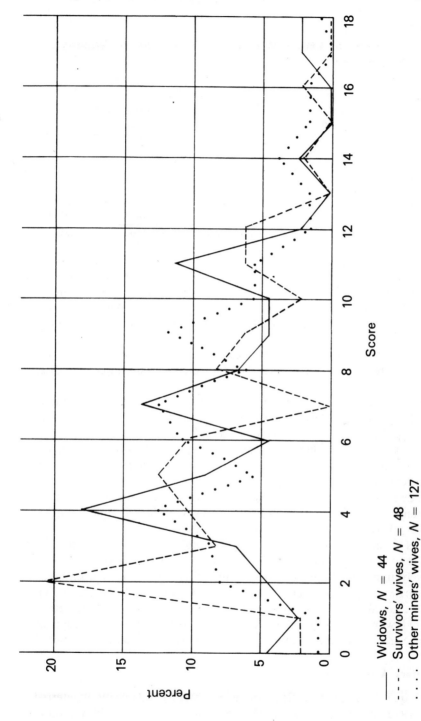

Includes telephone calls and personal visits with friends and relatives.

Figure 4-2. Distribution of Summary Social Contact Scores

Table 4-1
Number of Personal Letters Written per Week, Chicago Widows and Kellogg Respondents
(percent)

| | | Kellogg Respondents | | |
| | | *Survivors'* | *Other Miners* | *Chicago* |
Number of Letters	*Widows*	*Wives*	*Wives*	*Widows*[a]
None	48	37	45	51
1-2	26	40	38	27
3-4	12	14	13	12
5-6	7	8	2	6
7-8	0	0	2	2
9 or more	7	2	0	3
(*N*)	(42)	(49)	(128)	(300)

[a]Helena Znaneicki Lopata, *Widowhood in an American City* (Cambridge, Mass.: Schenkman, 1973), p. 316.

a letter in the previous week; there is a slight but not statistically significant tendency for the widows to write numerous letters (7 percent wrote nine or more, compared to 2 percent of the survivors' wives and none of the other miners' wives). Stated in more positive terms, over half of the women in all three samples wrote one or more personal letters in the week preceding the interview. About one fourth (slightly less than the other miners' wives) were writing a letter at least every other day; they produced no fewer than three or four a week.

We have also included in table 4-1 a column for the Chicago widows whose letter-writing frequency is described by Lopata (1973:135, 292, 316). There is a slight difference in the question asked, for Lopata's referred to "an average week" rather than the preceding one. Writing without the benefit of comparison samples, Lopata concluded that letter writing was an insignificant form of interaction, for the widows' low level of written correspondence meant that most "make no effort toward active involvement in this manner in the lives of people living far away, be it their children, other relatives, or friends" (Lopata 1973:135).

It is remarkable to us how closely Lopata's percentages parallel our own. It may not be, as she seemed to imply, that Chicago widows are relatively uninvolved correspondents but rather that nobody does much letter writing these days. The scores for the Chicago widows seem about average; certainly they compare well with those of the younger, better-educated women we studied in Kellogg. Widows, either in Chicago or Kellogg, are as involved as other women in personal exchanges by mail.

Voluntary Associations

All the questions about participation in community organizations referred to the 1972 interview, and we generalize about change since widowhood in chapter 8 with the restudy. If the organizational involvement of the widows in 1972 were sharply distinct from that of the other women, some inferences about changes in affiliation might be justified, especially in view of the similarity between the widows and the others in the maintenance of kinship and friendship ties.

Glick suggests that most widows reestablish social linkages fairly early in the process of adjustment to their new status, and, "By the end of the first year of bereavement, most widows had returned to fairly active social participation" (Glick, Weiss, and Parkes 1974:222). Our data from the Sunshine widows suggest that the process may be well advanced by six months. Anticipating that the widows would reveal the oft-reported perceptions of being left out of things, we asked, "Are you as involved in community life as you would like to be?" Approximately two thirds of the women in all three samples said yes. Rather than the widows expressing feelings of abandonment and alienation, we find that in all three samples about one third of the women are less involved than they would prefer. In fact, the lowest rate of satisfaction with present community involvement was expressed by the survivors' wives (59 percent).

Even if the widows do not feel left out of community activities, it does not necessarily mean that their participation in voluntary associations is comparable to that of other women. Rather, in line with the replacement mode of widowhood, we might expect certain types of affiliation to be expanded. In other words, widows might be "abnormally" active in organizations because they were compensating for the missing marital roles with increased community activity.

A series of seven questions probed for membership in the various kinds of voluntary associations, and there were two additional items on involvement in organizational leadership. The questions, together with the proportions of women reporting one or more affiliations of each type, are given in table 4-2. The figures presented there reveal no evidence that the widows are disaffiliated with respect to voluntary associations; on the contrary, they are at least as likely as women in the other samples to belong and to participate. In every case but two, widows' rates for organizational affiliation are slightly higher than those for the survivors' wives. Most of the differences are small; the largest is a 17-point differential between the widows and the survivors' wives in recreational group membership. The widows are more apt to belong to recreational organizations such as bridge clubs or bowling leagues. There is also a slight tendency for the widows to be underrepresented among the officers of organizations. Other than these differences, widows are affiliated in approximately the same degree as the other women.

Reports about belonging to organizations do not reflect the degree of involvement in them. For example, a woman might pay her dues and be listed on a membership roster but never attend meetings. We had one question on participation, in addition to the two on leadership activity already noted. It read, "In the last month how many meetings did you go to, in-

Table 4-2
Memberships in Voluntary Associations, by Type of Organization

Type of Organization	*Percentage Reporting One or More Memberships*					
	Widows		*Survivors' Wives*		*Other Miners' Wives*	
	%	*(N)*	*%*	*(N)*	*%*	*(N)*
Are you a member of any:						
Fellowship organizations like Eastern Star, Rebeccas, the D.A.R.?	17	(42)	6	(50)	16	(128)
Labor unions or professional associations	12	(42)	8	(49)	6	(127)
Political organizations or action groups?	5	(43)	0	(50)	5	(128)
Recreational or social groups like an athletic team, a bridge or card club, bowling league, or any others?	29	(42)	12	(50)	20	(127)
Hobby groups, music groups, art or drama circles?	9	(43)	10	(50)	7	(127)
Community or neighborhood organizations like PTA, Red Cross, Jaycettes, or volunteer organizations?	19	(43)	18	(50)	24	(126)
Other type of organization?	14	(42)	12	(48)	14	(126)
Are you an officer in any of these organizations?	18	(38)	27	(41)	29	(98)
Do you serve on any special committees	29	(38)	19	(42)	35	(102)

Note: Number of cases (*N*) forming the base for each percentage is given in parentheses. Persons who belonged to no organizations were not included in base figures for questions on organizational leadership or committee service.

cluding committee meetings?'' Fifty percent of the widows said they had attended at least one meeting in the past month, compared to 35 percent for each of the other groups. The widows were also more apt to attend many meetings during the month. Twenty-four percent of them attended five or more meetings in the month prior to the interview, compared to only 2 percent and 16 percent, respectively, of the women in the other samples. The widows seemed to be more active in organizations than were the women in the comparison samples, in sum.

Comparisons of the number of associations respondents belonged to before widowhood and at the time of interview (averaging 11.5 years later) by Lopata (1973:248-249) led her to conclude that widowhood was accompanied by a decline in membership and active involvement in voluntary associations. She noted that the decline in memberships also seemed to ac-company aging itself, however, and it is difficult from her data to estimate how much of the apparent decline is due to aging or other causes and how much due to the status of widowhood.

In fact, this issue illustrates the problems of using Lopata's sample of Chicago widows as a comparison group in the present study. The dif-ferences between the samples are substantial. The Chicago widows were chosen by a quota system to include half aged 50-64 and half 65 and over, and so they are much older than the women in the Kellogg samples. Very few of the Chicago widows were widowed while young; 83 percent were at least 45 when widowed, and most had been widowed well over a decade when they were interviewed. In addition, the Chicago widows were less well educated, much more apt to be Catholic or Jewish and vastly different in husbands' and fathers' occupations.

In our own samples there is no evidence of widowhood being accom-panied by a decline in membership or activity in voluntary associations. As the distributions in table 4-3 demonstrate, widows are as likely as the sur-vivors' wives to have no memberships at all, and they are somewhat more likely to belong to three or more organizations.

One of the primary conclusions from Lopata's analysis of community involvement among Chicago widows was that "the educational achieve-ment of the widow and of her late husband . . . influences heavily the widow's participation in her community, whether through neighboring, voluntary associations, or work" (Lopata 1973:248-249, 262). Our own research corroborates Lopata's conclusion about the primacy of the wife's

Table 4-3
Number of Memberships in Voluntary Associations for Chicago Widows and Kellogg Respondents
(percent)

| | Kellogg Respondents | | | |
| | | Survivors' | Other Miners | Chicago |
Number of Memberships	Widows	Wives	Wives	Widows[a]
0	51	54	42	63
1	21	22	32	24
2	14	18	13	24
3	12	6	9	13
4	2	—	2	13
5	—	—	2	13
6	—	—	1	13
(N)	(43)	(50)	(127)	(301)

[a]Helena Znaneiki Lopata, *Widowhood in an American City* (Cambridge, Mass.: Schenkman, 1973), p. 249.

educational attainment as a predictor of participation in community activities.

The strong influence of her education on whether a woman belongs to and participates actively in voluntary associations is documented in table 4-4, which shows for each of four levels of education (grade school, some high school, high school graduate, and beyond high school) the proportion of women who reported neither memberships nor attendance at meetings in the month before the interview. For membership the pattern is consistent and sharp: the percent belonging to a voluntary association progressively increases (or, conversely, the proportion of disaffiliates decreases) with each increase in level of education. Among women who have gone beyond high school only a small fraction, between one seventh and one fifth, report no memberships, while among those with grade school educations or less, disaffiliation is the norm, with between 62 and 80 percent reporting no memberships. The pattern appears in all three samples, and it is not noticeably stronger among the widows than the other women.

When meeting attendance rather than membership is the criterion, the differences are somewhat less dramatic. There is an occasional inconsistency in the middle categories, but the general trend is the same: The greater the educational attainment, the higher the probability of attendance at meetings. That the widows are similar to the other two samples in the relationship between education and affiliation or participation may be seen in the comparison of summary coefficients of statistical association (gammas) for the three samples for the relationship between education and membership (gammas, respectively, were .45, .41, and .28) and between education and attendance at meetings (.30, .44, and .24). These moderately strong gammas, all positive, mean that in all samples the likelihood of meeting attendance or membership goes up with years of education. Note also that in each case the figure for the widows (the first coefficient) is very close to that for at least one of the two comparison samples. In the influence of education on affiliation in voluntary associations, the widows are like other women.

In view of the strong positive association between women's education and their memberships in voluntary associations, we should emphasize that the Sunshine Mine widows were somewhat *less* educated than the women in the other samples. There is therefore additional reason for interpreting their comparable affiliation levels and higher levels of meeting attendance as evidence of adjustment replacement behavior.

In summary, the widows do not perceive themselves to be isolated or uninvolved in community activities. Their rates of affiliation in organizations are as high or higher than those for the other women, and judging from a single item on meeting attendance, they are more apt to participate actively in the organizations to which they belong.

Table 4-4
Nonmembership and Nonparticipation in Voluntary Associations, by Education

| Education | Percent Reporting No Memberships | | | | | | Percent Reporting No Meeting Attended in Past Month | | | | | |
| | Widows | | Survivors' Wives | | Other Miners' Wives | | Widows | | Survivors' Wives | | Other Miners' Wives | |
	%	(N)	%	(N)	%	(N)	%	(N)	%	(N)	%	(N)
0-8	67	(6)	80	(5)	62	(24)	67	(6)	100	(5)	90	(21)
9-11	64	(22)	68	(19)	42	(43)	46	(22)	72	(18)	56	(39)
12	38	(8)	47	(17)	37	(46)	71	(7)	53	(17)	62	(45)
13+	14	(7)	22	(9)	21	(14)	29	(7)	38	(8)	42	(12)
(N)		(43)		(50)		(127)		(42)		(48)		(117)

Note: Number of cases forming the base for each percentage is given in parentheses.

One way the widows might use membership in voluntary associations to help them adjust would be for the organization to serve as a setting where new friendships were made. If it served that purpose, then the widows who had acquired new friends should be overrepresented among those active in organizations. Accordingly, we compared the widows who belonged to one or more organizations with those who did not for the item, "Since the mine disaster, has your group of friends changed?" Results of this tabulation provided strong evidence for the role of community organizations as contexts for finding and maintaining the new friendships for widows. Among the other miners' wives, 16 percent of those who belonged to an organization said that their group of friends had changed, but so did 14 percent of the women who did not belong. Comparable figures for the survivors' wives were 29 percent and 27 percent. Thus whether they belonged to organizations had no effect on friendship changes among the women in the comparison samples. Among the widows there was a striking differential: 56 percent of those who were affiliated said their group of friends had changed, compared to only 38 percent of those who did not belong to an organization. For the other miners' wives and the survivors' wives, the turnover in friendships was the same, independent of membership in an organization. For the widows a change in friendships was much more likely if the woman belonged to an organization than if she did not belong. An organization thus seems to serve as a contextual or mediating group, aiding the widow in adjustment to widowhood by replacement of friends.

Religion and Church Activity

Disasters emphasize the relative importance of human communities, and they can set people to examining relationships to the sacred or the supernatural. Between 86 and 91 percent of the women in the three samples said that during the week of the search for the missing men they prayed or felt the need to pray. Moreover, the clergy and church organizations were highly visible in administering aid and attempting to comfort relatives and friends of the victims. Much less visible and more problematic is the role of organized religion as an aid to the widows during the months following the disaster.

In order to explore the women's involvement in organized religion, it was necessary to distinguish several dimensions of religiosity. First, there is the salience of religion (Bahr, Bartel, and Chadwick 1972) or its rank of importance as compared to other aspects of a person's life. Three questions in the interview schedule had to do with the salience of religion. One asked the respondent to assess how religious she was, on a scale ranging from "very religious" to "not at all religious." A second question focused on church membership, and, like the first, it referred to the respondent's feelings at the time of interview: "All in all, how important would you say your church membership is to you?" The last question put present levels of religious salience in the context of experiences the woman had had during the past six months: "Do you feel that your religion has gained or lost importance since the disaster?" Responses to these questions are summarized in table 4-5.

A disaster might influence people's religious behavior by increasing their feelings of need for supernatural aid, by increasing their sense of investment in a life beyond (where they believe a loved one may be waiting), or by increasing awareness of their own mortality (the "there are no atheists in foxholes" syndrome). Each of these types of influence would be expected to increase the attitudinal commitment and the religious activity. Glick, Weiss, and Parkes (1974:133-134) report that religious beliefs helped to sustain morale following the initial period of intense grief. Approximately three fourths of the widows they interviewed affirmed that their spouses' deaths had not changed their religious beliefs, and a majority (59 percent) said that their religious beliefs were a source of comfort in adjusting to bereavement.

The influence of disaster-related religious attitudes ought to be greatest among those most directly affected by the event (the widows) and least among those for whom the disaster was less of a personal trauma (the other miners' wives). We would expect the survivors' wives, who in effect occupy a middle ground, touched not bereaved by the disaster, to exhibit an increased influence of religion, but not as much as the widows.

Another way a disaster may affect religiosity is the "curse God and die" effect. In this adaptation a widow who prayed for the safety of her man but was disappointed might abandon her relgious ideals and withdraw from "affiliation" with the supernatural or its alleged earthly representatives. Such withdrawal would reflect the apparent inability of those representatives or the apparent unwillingness of Providence to answer her prayers. If this adaptation occurred, we would anticipate that the widows would exhibit the greatest change and the other miners' wives the least change, but the direction of the change would be toward *less* commitment and church activity rather than more. There is some previous work (Glick, Weiss, and Parkes 1974:133) suggesting that as many as one out of eight widows see their bereavement as damaging to their religious faith.

The results in table 4-5 suggest that both types of religious adaptation to disaster were operating among the Sunshine widows. They were more likely than the other women to say that they were "very religious," and both the widows and the survivors' wives were more likely than the other miners' wives to say that their church membership was "extremely important" to them. Most revealing, however, is the item on whether or not the importance of religion has changed since the disaster. Substantial proportions of

Table 4-5

Distribution of Responses to Questions on Church Activity and the Salience of Religion

Indicators of Church Activity and Salience of Religion	Widows	Survivors' Wives	Other Miners' Wives
We know that some people are more religious than others. Do you feel that you are very religious, religious, somewhat religious, not very religious, or not at all religious?			
Very religious	30	18	23
Somewhat religious	60	68	64
Not very or not at all religious	9	14	13
(N)	(43)	(50)	(128)
All in all, how important would you say your church membership is to you?[a]			
Extremely important	54	55	40
Quite important or fairly important	32	40	51
Not too important	14	5	9
(N)	(28)	(20)	(77)
Do you feel that your religion has gained or lost importance since the disaster?			
Gained importance	52	43	34
Stayed the same	32	53	65
Lost importance	16	4	1
(N)	(44)	(49)	(125)
How often do you attend worship services?			
Every week	32	22	28
Nearly every week or at least once a month	32	24	24
At least once a year	18	28	22
Never	18	26	26
(N)	(44)	(50)	(128)
Thinking of the frequency of your attendance now as compared to before the disaster, would you say you attend church more now or less now than you did before the disaster?[b]			
More now	16	19	7
About the same	54	68	88
Less now	30	13	5
(N)	(37)	(31)	(96)
Do you participate in any church groups and their social events?			
Percent saying yes	36	23	31
(N)	(44)	(43)	(123)

Approximately how many evenings a week are

Table 4-5 *(Continued)*

Indicators of Church Activity and Salience of Religion	Widows	Survivors' Wives	Other Miners' Wives
spent in church activities or in church study groups?[c]			
Two or more	44	56	32
One	37	33	47
None	19	11	21
(N)	(16)	(9)	(38)

[a]This question was asked only of women who said they were members of a church.

[b]This question was not asked of those who had responded that they "never" attended worship services.

[c]This question was asked only of those who had responded that they did participate in church groups and their social events.

all three samples (34 percent of the other miners' wives, 43 percent of the survivors' wives, and 52 percent of the widows) reported an increased importance of religion in their lives. As anticipated, the proportion of those reporting an increase varied directly with the closeness of the disaster to the respondent. That is, increased religious salience was most common among the widows, somewhat less common among the survivors' wives, and least common among the other miners' wives.

The most striking thing about the figures in table 4-5 is the reported *decrease* in salience of religion among one sixth of the widows, which is not matched in either of the other samples. Only 1 percent of the other miners' wives reported a decline in salience of religion, suggesting that the reasons for the decline among the widows are indeed tied to the disaster and to the experience of widowhood. Note also, however, that even though one widow in six said that religion had lost importance in her life, the widows as a whole still view themselves as more religious than do the survivors' wives or the other miners' wives.

Another way to study the effects of the disaster on religious involvement is to examine reports of behavior rather than attitudes and values. The interview schedule focused on one dimension of religious behavior, that of church attendance. There were four questions about different aspects of church attendance. Two had to do with attendance at worship services, another treated participation in church social events, and the last asked for a rough estimate of the amount of time spent in church activities. The questions and distribution of responses to them are given in the lower part of table 4-5.

The influence of the disaster both to increase and to decrease church attendance parallels its influence on perceptions of the importance of religion in the women's lives. The results in table 4-5 show that while the widows attend church more frequently than the other women, a substantial number of them (30 percent) say that since the disaster they attend church less than formerly. On the other hand, both among the widows and the survivors' wives a sizeable proportion (between one sixth and one fifth) report that they attend church more frequently now than they did before the disaster.

The most important finding in this regard is the apparent influence of the disaster on the religious attitudes and behaviors of those most touched by the disaster, namely, the widows and the survivors' wives. Both these groups of women appeared to have experienced significant change in their religious lives as a consequence of the Sunshire fire. A situation of stability or relative continuity in attitudes applied to only one third of the widows and half of the survivors' wives, and there was also marked instability in attendance patterns, although these differences were not as great as for religious attitudes.

To state this another way: two thirds of the widows said their religious attitudes had changed; but for the comparison sample of other miners' wives, two thirds reported stability, not change. With respect to church attendance almost half of the widows reported change compared to only 12 percent of the other miners' wives. In each case the survivors' wives occupied an intermediate position, showing considerably more change than the other miners' wives but less than the widows.

Summary

Widows' reports of their social interaction and activity in voluntary associations and our exploration of widows' reports of their contacts with friends and relatives, voluntary associations, and churches lead to several conclusions. First, with respect to amount of interaction with friends and relatives and activity in voluntary associations, the widows at six months after bereavement were very similar to other women. Such a consistent similarity suggests the operation of two modes of adjustment to widowhood, continuity and replacement. This is not to say that there has not been some withdrawal disaffiliation as well; as was pointed out, the three types of adaptation may succeed each other in the experience of one woman, and it is probable that withdrawal disaffiliation is the dominant mode of adaptation for a few. After all, 5 percent of the widows said at interview that they had fewer friends than they had had before widowhood, and hence on the friendship dimension we may say definitely that 5 percent manifested a withdrawal disaffiliation adjustment.

For interaction with relatives and activity in voluntary associations, we cannot provide exact percentages of those whose experiences fit the withdrawal disaffiliation mode, but the high congruity between the widows and the other samples in contact with relatives and organizational affiliation argues against those percentages being very high. Instead, the intensification of existing ties or their replacement with new ones seems to have been the dominant type of adaptation.

It is in religious activity and belief that the widows seem most sharply distinct from the other women. The disaster seems to have had a definite effect on the widows' personal religiosity. At times that took a direction toward greater involvement and participation in religious activity (a replacement trend), and less frequently it showed a decline in both degree of religious activity and perceived personal salience of religious life (a withdrawal disaffiliation trend).

The dominant modes of adaptation are clearly continuity and replacement, and for those types of interaction and affiliation where we have statistical estimates, the probability that one of these two modes will obtain ranges from 70 percent to 95 percent. Because our analysis has taken each type of interaction or social activity separately, we are unable at this point to characterize a global "direction in life organization" adaptation, as did Glick, Weiss, and Parkes (1974:233-253). Adaptation to widowhood is multifaceted, and there is no reason why the widow whose friendship adaptation has been a withdrawal disaffiliation mode should manifest that same mode in her relationships with relatives or with the church. Nevertheless, some contrasts between the alternate directions in life organization of Glick and his associates and an impressionistic summary of the evidence presented in this chapter may be of interest. It will be recalled that the 47 widows for whom Glick, Weiss, and Parkes had sufficient data to permit a global categorization by type of life adjustment fell into five categories; we have grouped these in table 4-6 to correspond to our own three categories.

Six months after widowhood most of the women widowed in the Sunshine Mine fire were maintaining ties to friends, relatives, and voluntary associations at about the same level as were other women in the community. They had achieved this by continuing and perhaps intensifying relationships that existed before the fire or by establishing new ties. A small proportion were isolated in one or more ways, but so were a few women in the comparison samples. The widows were not affiliated or perfectly adjusted before the fire, and it would be a mistake to blame their widowhood for the continuing isolation or disaffiliation of some of them. Our use of comparison samples has permitted us to identify the normal levels of social isolation and disaffiliation among women in the Kellogg community, and to see how the widows' involvement in the social network differs from that reported by other women rather than from some ideal level of affiliation

Table 4-6
Contrasts in the Incidence of Selected Modes of Adjustment to Widowhood

Patterns of Involvement in the Social Network, Kellogg Widows		"Alternative Directions in Life Organizations"[b]	
Type	Estimated Incidence[a] (%)	Type	Estimated Incidence (%)
Continuity	30-50	—[c]	—
		Independence from close relationships with other adults	36
Withdrawal disaffiliation	5-30	Chaotic life organization, or failure to move toward reorganization of a stable life pattern	13
		Movement toward remarriage	30
Replacement	15-55	Nonmarital relationship with a man	11
		Kin-centered life organization	11

[a]Varies by type of social involvement considered, such as contact with relatives or friends or participation in voluntary associations.

[b]Ira O. Glick, Robert S. Weiss, and C. Murray Parkes, *The First Year of Bereavement* (New York: Wiley, 1974).

[c]No counterpart in Glick, Weiss, and Parkes 1974.

and adjustment. In the main the Sunshine Mine widows seem to have been very successful in maintaining or reachieving normal levels of social interaction and activity.

References

Atchley, Robert C. 1975. "Dimensions of Widowhood in Later Life." *The Gerontologist* 15 (April):176-178.

Bahr, Howard M., Bartel, Lois Franz, and Chadwick, Bruce A. 1971. "Orthodoxy, Activism, and the Salience of Religion." *Journal for the Scientific Study of Religion* 10 (Summer):69-75.

Berardo, Felix. 1967. "Social Adaptation to Widowhood Among a Rural-Urban Aged Population." *Washington Agricultural Experiment Station Bulletin 689*, College of Agriculture, Washington State University.

Bock, E. Wilbur, and Webber, Irving L. 1972. "Suicide Among the Elderly: Isolating Widowhood and Mitigating Alternatives." *Journal of Marriage and the Family* 34 (February):24-31.

Bornstein, Philipp E., Clayton, Paula J., Halikas, James A., Maurice, William L., and Robins, Eli. 1973. "The Depression of Widowhood

After Thirteen Months." *British Journal of Psychiatry* 122 (May):561-566.

Briscoe, C. William, and Smith, James B. 1975. "Depression in Bereavement and Divorce," *Archives of General Psychiatry* 32 (April):439-443.

Caine, Lynn. 1974. *Widow*. New York: Morrow.

Carey, Raymond G. 1977. "The Widowed: A Year Later." *Journal of Counseling Psychology* 24 (no. 2):125-131.

Clayton, Paula J. 1973. "The Clinical Morbidity of the First Year of Bereavement: A Review." *Comprehensive Psychiatry* 14 (March/April):151-157.

_____ . 1974. "Mortality and Morbidity in the First Year of Widowhood."*Archives of General Psychiatry* 30 (June):747-750.

Clayton, Paula J., Halikas, James A., and Maurice, William L. 1972. "The Depression of Widowhood." *British Journal of Psychiatry* 120 (January):71-78.

Clayton, Paula J., Halikas, James A., Maurice, Wiliam L., and Robins, Eli. 1973. "Anticipatory Grief and Widowhood." *British Journal of Psychiatry* 122 (January):47-51.

Glick, Ira O., Weiss, Robert S., and Parkes, C. Murray. 1974. *The First Year of Bereavement*. New York: Wiley.

Gubrium, Jaber F. 1974. "Marital Desolation and the Evaluation of Everyday Life in Old Age," *Journal of Marriage and the Family* 36 (February):107-113.

Harvey, Carol D., and Bahr, Howard M. 1974. "Widowhood, Morale, and Affiliation." *Journal of Marriage and the Family* 36 (February):97-106.

Lewis, Alfred Allan. 1975. *Three Out of Four Wives*. New York: Macmillan.

Lopata, Helena Znaneicki. 1970. "The Social Involvement of American Widows." *American Behavioral Scientist* 14 (September/October):41-57.

_____ . 1972. "Social Relations of Widows in Urbanizing Societies." *Sociological Quarterly* 13 (Spring):259-271.

_____ . 1973. *Widowhood in an American City*. Cambridge, Mass.: Schenkman.

McCourt, William F., Barnett, Ruth D., Brennen, Jean, and Becker, Alvin. 1976."We Help Each Other: Primary Prevention for the Widowed." *American Journal of Psychiatry* 133 (January):98-100.

Parkes, C. Murray, and Brown, R.J. 1972. "Health After Bereavement: A Controlled Study of Young Boston Widows and Widowers." *Psychosomatic Medicine* 34 (September/October):449-461.

Walker, Kenneth N., MacBride, Arlene, and Vachon, Mary L.S. 1977. "Social Support Networks and the Crisis of Bereavement." *Social Science and Medicine* 11:35-41.

5 Personal Reactions: Morale, Happiness, and Outlook

Questions about ties to friends, relatives, and community organizations all pertain to the network that binds a person to others outside the self. Perhaps as important, however, are questions about a person's feelings about self and how these change in response to crisis or loss. These are sometimes designated as psychological aspects, in contrast to the more strictly social dimensions of adjustment. In this chapter we will consider several aspects of the personal morale of the newly widowed, including the widows' perceptions of changes in their attitudes since the Sunshine fire and comparisons between the groups on a number of indicators of psychological attitude at the time of the interview.

The personal reactions to widowhood are perhaps the best documented aspects of the process of adjustment to bereavement. An identification of stages of bereavement was published in the early years of the 1930s (Eliot 1930a; 1930b; 1932) and extended in the early 1940s (Fulconer 1942). Studies of emotional reactions to widowhood have a longer history, beginning with Freud's work on the psychodynamics of grief (Freud 1917). The British psychiatrist Colin Murray Parkes is quoted as saying, "I know of only one functional psychiatric disorder whose cause is known, whose features are distinctive and whose course is usually predictable. And that is grief, the reaction to loss" (Caine 1974:89).

This is not the place for an extensive review of the literature on reactions to grief; Switzer's (1970) book *The Dynamics of Grief* devotes an entire chapter to a review of the literature on the concept of grief, noting that while grief has received relatively little attention compared to many other human emotions, there have been substantial contributions from the fields of psychology, psychoanalysis, medicine, and pastoral care (Switzer 1970:19-20). Let us briefly outline the stages of adjustment that have been identified.

One description of the stages of grief is cast in terms of "psychological responses" and includes (1) thought and behavior directed toward the lost object, (2) hostility, guilt, and feelings of unworthiness, (3) appeals for help, (4) despair, withdrawal, regression, disorganization, and feelings of futility and emptiness, and finally (5) reorganization of behavior directed toward new relationships (Switzer 1970:43-44; see also Bowlby, 1960, 1969, 1973).

In another widely used model (Fulconer 1942; Nye and Berardo 1973:594-598), there are said to be four stages of adjustment to bereavement: immediate, postimmediate, transitional, and repatterning stages.

Types of response in the immediate stage include stoicism, dazedness, collapse, and the lachrymose. During the postimmediate, which lasts until the end of the funeral activities, responses include acquiescence, excitement, protestive behavior, detachment, and despondency. The transitional stage extends from first adjustments to the suffering of loss until established adjustive patterns are integrated into a new life pattern. It includes the responses of alternating between high and low levels of activity and morale, the enforced-collaborative responses in which there is a return to necessary duties and relationships, and attention-seeking behavior. Finally, the repatterning stage involves resumption of "normal" life and development of a stable life pattern. It is characterized by projective responses, emphasis on increased participation, identification with the roles of the deceased along with an emphasis on "doing something," considerable emphasis on memory and fantasy, and some degree of repressive-seclusive behavior in which the bereaved person holds him/herself aloof from certain normal contacts and activities. The duration of each stage varies, but by six months after bereavement, most persons would be considered in the repatterning stage, and that is the stage we will assume the widowed respondents to be experiencing.

To these psychological and sociological insights about grief may be added the medical research, which generally has found that grief disturbs the person's total adjustment and may be a factor contributing to a variety of psychological problems and medical conditions. Switzer's own synthesis of the perspectives of these various disciplines emphasizes that because the development of the self depends in part on interaction with significant others. Consequently, loss of one significant other represents loss of part of one's own personality, and it is necessarily accompanied by pain and damage to the emotional life (Switzer 1970:46, 60).

Contrasts in Personal Morale

Although it may be temporary, the damage to self that follows widowhood has repeatedly been shown to affect both physical and mental health. Women do respond to bereavement in different ways; the degree of impairment in mental or physical health may be influenced by a widow's age, education, employment status, the presence of children at home, ethnic background, and religious affiliation (Barrett 1977:863-864). At least three sets of factors influence the impact of bereavement. The first are characteristics of the widow herself such as those just mentioned. Second, there are the circumstances surrounding her husband's death. (Was it sudden or expected? What was her morale before that time? Was a supportive network of family and friends available? Were there others who shared a similar loss?) Finally, the characteristics of the period between the bereavement and the measurement of personal morale or health are important. (How long has it been? What stages of the process of adjusting to grief has the widow worked through? What replacements have there been for the role activities formerly carried out by the deceased husband?) Also relevant is the community context in which a widow's morale is measured. (Is she presently residing in the same community where she and her husband lived? Have numerous economic and social factors operated to bring about a residential concentration of widows who have a variety of backgrounds and experiences?)

Generally the comparisons between widows and married women that have produced many of the findings on the consequences of widowhood have taken few intervening factors into account. A serious consequence of this lack of control by researchers over potentially significant intervening factors is the probability that some of the negative consequences attributed to the status of widowhood derive from other characteristics of the women being studied. For example, an analysis of the linkage between widowhood status and low morale in five nations suggests that "the negative impact" sometimes attributed to widowhood derives not from widowhood status but rather from socioeconomic status. The widowed have appeared to have more negative attitudes than the married because they are much poorer than the married (Harvey and Bahr 1974:106). This finding does not mean that widowhood status has no effect upon morale but rather that its effects seem less devastating than those of poverty. Among widows of all ages, most of whom have been widowed for long periods, "studies which have attributed long-term . . . demoralizing consequences to widowhood should be reassessed to be sure that controls for income level have been adequate" (Harvey and Bahr 1974:106). The same logic applies to all the intervening variables listed above.

Among the prime justifications for the study of the Sunshine widows is the extraordinary control over many intervening variables that the situation permits. There are two main ways to deal with the possible errors introduced by such uncontrolled factors. One is to measure as many of them as possible and to deal with them statistically in the course of the analysis. For example, grouping widows into homogeneous categories by age, length of time widowed, or level of education are ways to "control" the effects of age, duration, or education. The problem with this approach is that one never manages to control for all the possible intervening factors. The pragmatics of the situation may prevent it; moreover, there simply may not be enough widows of a given age or education. The other way is to sidestep the need to measure each respondent's unique characteristics by finding a relatively homogeneous sample in which there is a heightened probability that an unmeasured characteristic is shared by many of the respondents. The widows of the Sunshine Mine fire comprise such a homogeneous group. They were widowed at the same time, their husbands followed the same oc-cupation and worked for the same company, they lived in the same small towns, and their bereavements were sudden and unanticipated. The nature of the situation therefore provides built-in controls for these or other in-tervening variables that may have affected morale in widowhood.

Whatever the state of adjustment in which the widows of the Sunshine miners happened to be when interviewed, according to prior research on bereavement and to social psychological theory about the development and maintenance of the self, they ought to manifest lower morale than the women in the other two samples. As anticipated, the psychological costs of widowhood show up in the women's responses to questions about worry and personal happiness. The widows are most apt to say they worry a lot, and they are much more likely to report that they worry more now than formerly. Seventy percent of them (compared to 34 percent of survivors' wives) said that they worried differently now than a year ago; over half of the widows were "not too happy," in contrast to only 12 and 9 percent, respectively, of the other samples of women (see table 5-1). The widows are three times more likely than the other women to say that they are "not do-ing too well now," and they are between two and three times more likely to indicate dissatisfaction with life by wanting to "change many parts of it."

The third item in table 5-1 has a lengthy history as an indicator of overall life quality. It was first used in 1957 by Gurin, Veroff, and Feld (1960); later it was included in several national surveys. By contrasting the Kellogg women's responses with those for national surveys, we can get some idea about how typical our respondents are. Rodgers and Converse (1975) showed trends in reported happiness based on six studies conducted be-tween 1957 and 1972, all of which had used this item. They found a decline in the proportion claiming to be "very happy" but little change in the pro-portion who claimed to be "not too happy." The unhappy were usually be-tween 9 and 11 percent of the respondents, although in two national quota samples the proportion rose to one sixth.

A 1972 national study conducted by the University of Michigan Survey Research Center at roughly the same time as our interview of Kellogg widows provides a context against which our findings may be viewed.

Twenty-two percent of the national sample said that they were "very happy," 68 percent were "pretty happy," and 10 percent were "not too happy" when questioned by Michigan researchers. The survivors' wives and other miners' wives in the Kellogg samples were somewhat more likely to say they were "very happy" (42 percent and 34 percent, respectively) than was the average American adult in 1972, but in the "not too happy" category, they were similar to the national figures (12 percent and 9

Table 5-1
Reports of Worry, Happiness, and Personal Outlook

Item	Widows	Survivors' Wives	Other Miners' Wives
In general, do you spend a lot of time worrying, not very much time, or do you not worry at all?			
Percent "a lot"	50	40	35
(N)	(44)	(50)	(126)
Do you worry now differently than you did a year ago? That is, do you worry more, less, or about the same?			
Percent "more"	70	34	23
(N)	(44)	(50)	(128)
Taken all together, how would you say things are these days—would you say you are very happy, relatively happy, or not too happy?			
Percent "not too happy"	56	12	9
(N)	(43)	(50)	(128)
When you think of the things you want from life, would you say that you're doing pretty well or not doing too well now in getting the things you want?			
Percent "not doing too well"	26	8	8
(N)	(42)	(48)	(118)
Think of how your life is going now. Do you want it to continue in much the same way as it is going now; do you wish you could change some parts of it; or do you wish you could change many parts of it?			
Percent "change many parts"	26	12	9
Percent "continue in much the same way"	12	30	36
(N)	(43)	(50)	(128)

percent). In contrast, the widows appear as a markedly depressed group. Almost 60 percent of them, six times as many as either the Kellogg comparison groups or the national sample, placed themselves in the "not too happy" category.

Positive and Negative Outlook

Bradburn's (1969) *The Structure of Psychological Well-Being* used evidence from several large-scale surveys of metropolitan areas to assess levels of morale in the general population. The indicators of "well-being" were designed to reflect people's experience with different experiences, and yet were general enough to apply to the population at large. There were two major "waves" of the Bradburn surveys, Wave I conducted in January and February of 1963 and Wave III the following October and November. Waves II and IV had much smaller samples and will not be considered here.

In both major waves Bradburn's composite sampling frame included suburban and inner-city Detroit, Chicago, a suburban county near Washington, D.C., and residents in the ten largest metropolitan areas in the country. The distribution of answers of people drawn in the sample of these areas is given in table 5-2. In his discussion of how people answered the questions on positive and negative affect, Bradburn noted (1969:55-56) that they were more apt to say yes to the positive items than the negative ones; that is, people were much more apt to say that they were happy than that they were unhappy.

Bradburn's ten affect items were included in our interview schedule. By

Table 5-2
Reports of Positive and Negative Affect, Bradburn's Metropolitan Samples and Kellogg Women

During the past few weeks did you ever feel:	Bradburn, Wave I (1963)	Bradburn, Wave III (1963)	Kellogg Women (Survivors' and Other Miners' Wives (1972)	Kellogg Widows (1972)
Positive Feelings				
Pleased about having accomplished something?	78	77	85	82
That things were going your way?	64	70	83	70
Proud because someone complimented you on something you have done?	67	66	79	75
Particularly excited or interested in something?	56	57	77	68
On top of the world?	29	33	52	42
Negative Feelings				
So restless that you could not sit long in a chair?	48	30	51	80
Bored?	38	33	44	73
Depressed or very unhappy	33	30	44	86
Very lonely or remote from other people?	27	23	39	91
Upset because someone criticized you?	21	18	27	20
(N)	(2,787)	(2,163)	(178)[a]	(44)

Note: For the Bradburn surveys, the percentages represent those who answered yes; for the Kellogg surveys, which had a three-category response format rather than Bradburn's yes or no options, the percentages include women answering either "once" or "more than once."

[a]This is the modal N; for one item it was 173, and for four items it was 177.

comparing the Kellogg samples with his large metropolitan samples, we can get an idea of how perceptions of happiness among our respondents differ from the national patterns. Table 5-2 shows the distribution of responses by the Kellogg women as well as the findings reported by Bradburn. Remember that the data for Kellogg refer to females only while the comparison figures from Bradburn's surveys include responses from both sexes. Bradburn concluded that the differences between men and women, however, were slight and that in the general structure of psychological well-being revealed by responses to these ten items, there were no significant differences by sex (Bradburn 1969:69-61). Accordingly it is legitimate to compare our findings for Kellogg women with his for people generally.

There were slight differences between the wording of the Bradburn items and the ones we used. Bradburn asked, "During the past few weeks did you ever feel . . . " and had two standard responses, yes or no. Our question was limited to just "the past week," rather than the last few weeks, and there were three possible responses, "not at all," "once," and "more than once." However, the three-response format can be made comparable to Bradburn's yes-no approach by combining the latter two categories. That is what we have done to produce the percentages in table 5-2, with our "not at all" response corresponding to Bradburn's no, and the combined "once" and "more than once" correspoding to his yes.

The Kellogg women are more apt to report positive feelings than were people in the national surveys. Even the widows, among whom the reports of positive affect are slightly lower (not more than 10 percent) than among the other Kellogg women, show higher percentages with positive feelings than did the national surveys. Kellogg widows do not therefore appear to be atypical in their experience of positive feelings.

It is in negative feelings that the dramatic differences between widows and the other women appear. Kellogg women in all three samples are somewhat more apt to report negative feelings than are people in the national metropolitan samples. (Their rates range about 10-15 percent higher than in the metropolitan samples.) The widows are much more apt to report negative feelings than are people in the national samples. They are about twice as likely to say they are restless, bored, and depressed and three times as likely to be lonely. In fact more widows reported loneliness (91 percent) than any other negative feeling, and the difference between the widows and of either the other Kellogg women or the national samples was larger for the loneliness item than for any of the other negative feelings measured.

Comparison of the results for both positive feelings and negative feelings shows that the widows have their fair share of positive feelings, but they have much more than their share of negative feelings. The figures in table 5-2 demonstrate quite dramatically how choice of a particular type of attitude item may either mask or enhance intersample differences. If we concentrated only on the positive feelings, we would conclude that the widows were quite typical. It is in their high frequency of negative feelings, rather than in an absence of positive feelings, that they are atypical. Without the items on loneliness, depression, and restlessness, we might have concluded that the widows were better adjusted than they are.

Paying attention to both positive and negative feelings as indicators of morale leads logically to striking a balance between the two to arrive at some kind of overall summary. The problem is analogous to that which Condie and Doan (1978) confront in their conceptualization of "role profit," which is computed by subtracting role costs from role rewards. In the present situation the positive feeling items may not be similar enough to the negative ones to merit simple mathematical combination; for example, 40 percentage points of restlessness may not be comparable to the same proportion of responses indicating pleasure at accomplishment. The possibility of counterbalancing positive and negative feelings and thereby producing a net loss for the widows and a net profit for the other samples is clearly available from the data in table 5-2. Note, for example, that among the widows the proportions having negative feelings are generally about the same or larger than those reporting positive feelings, but reports of positive feelings, whatever the item, are usually much more frequent than reports of negative feelings, in comparison to the other samples.

Quantitative Estimates of Goodness of Life

Another approach to estimating people's general morale is to ask them to assign numbers to their own level of happiness or satisfaction. Overall estimates of quality of present life among the Kellogg women were obtained by a question that asked the women to rank their situation on a numerical scale ranging from 1 to 10. The interviewer showed each woman a picture of a ladder with numbers centered above each rung, saying,

> Here is a picture of a ladder. Suppose we say that the top of the ladder (10) represents the best possible life for you and the bottom (1) represents the worst possible life for you. Where on the ladder do you feel you personally stand at the present time? Step number _____ (Cantril 1966).

There were two subsequent questions in the same format, one that asked about the past and one about the future. ("Where on the ladder would you say you stood five years ago?" "And where do you think you will be on the ladder five years from now?")

Table 5-3 summarizes responses to these items, and it shows that the most striking contrasts between the widows and the other samples are not in present status but in perceptions of quality of life in the past. To highlight this idealization of the past by the widows, we drew the frequency polygons

Table 5-3

Percentage Distribution of Responses to the Quality of Life Question, for Present Life, Five Years Past, and Five Years in the Future

Here is a picture of a ladder. Suppose we say that the top of the ladder (10) represents the best possible life for you and the bottom (1) represents the worst possible life for you:

	Widows (%)	Survivors' Wives (%)	Other Miners' Wives (%)
Where on the ladder do you feel you personally stand at the present time?			
Step number			
0	—	—	—
1	14	—	—
2	—	—	1
3	—	6	1
4	9	2	2
5	27	20	17
6	18	18	11
7	18	16	26
8	7	22	27
9	5	8	6
10	2	8	10
Total	100	100	101
(*N*)	(44)	(50)	(128)
Where on the ladder would you say you stood five years ago?			
Step number			
0	—	2	1
1	2	2	12
2	2	8	9
3	5	14	9
4	2	16	9
5	9	22	15
6	11	6	18
7	5	4	9
8	7	16	13
9	20	4	3
10	36	6	3
Total	99	100	101
(*N*)	(44)	(50)	(127)
Where do you think you will be on the ladder five years from now?			
Step number			
0	—	—	1
1	3	2	—
2	—	—	—
3	—	—	—
4	3	2	1
5	10	8	6
6	3	2	4
7	8	10	15
8	13	20	23
9	21	14	14
10	40	41	36
Total	101	99	100
(*N*)	(38)	(49)	(126)

in figure 5-1, which contrast the present, past, and future estimates of quality of life for each sample.

The first panel of the figure portrays the widows' estimations of their present quality of life in a solid line, contrasted to the dashed line for the past (five years ago) and the dotted line for the future (five years from now). The modal response for the widows' estimates of present life quality is the midpoint of the scale (5), while for both of the other samples the modal response for the present is somewhat higher (8). The shape of the distribution for all three samples of women, as we contrast the solid line in the first panel with the solid line in the other panels of figure 5-1, is roughly the same, with one or more peaks in the center of the distribution and relatively few women claiming either very high or very low quality of life.

We therefore find that the estimations of the past by the survivors' wives and the other miners' wives are not much different from their views of the present. They tend to view the past as somewhat worse than the present but not dramatically so. In stark contrast to their pattern is the widows' profile for the past: Over 60 percent of the widows assessed their past life in such favorable terms that they accorded it scores of 8 or more on the 10-point scale.

Now inspect the dotted lines in figure 5-1, which represent the future. They show very little variation from sample to sample; almost everyone was optimistic about the future. It is notable that the widows' estimates of the level of past happiness are congruent with their favorable outlook for the future.

Miners' wives may be generally optimistic about future prospects, but they tend not to idealize the recent past. Widows, however, do idealize the past. Their exaggeration of past life quality, coupled with their present disadvantaged position, must increase their sense of deprivation and loss.

Let us emphasize once more that it is only the presence of data from the other two samples of women that makes it possible to be so certain about this idealization of the past by the widows. Without the comparison samples, we could only say that the widows view the past and the future as considerably happier than the present. With the data from the other women, it is possible to affirm that no group of miner's wives in Kellogg could have had lives as happy as the widows remember their recent past to have been.

Satisfaction with Specific Aspects of Life

Some clues to the nature of widows' morale may also be gleaned from questions about satisfaction with particular elements of present life, as opposed to the global, "all things considered" estimates of happiness. We asked the women how they felt about six aspects of their present life, family income, house and furniture, recreation, relationship to children, the community of

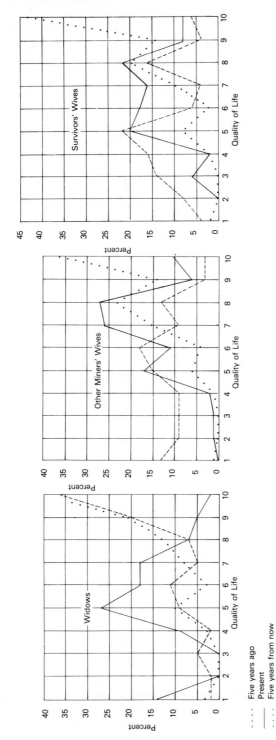

Note: The item read, "Here is a picture of a ladder. Suppose we say that the top of the ladder (10) represents the best possible life for you and the bottom (1) represents the worst possible life for you. Where on the ladder do you feel you personally stand at the present time? Step number _____?" Two subsequent probes asked for a position on the ladder "five years ago" and "five years from now."

Figure 5-1. Percentage Distribution by Perceived Quality of Life Five Years Ago, at Present, and Five Years in the Future

Kellogg, and daily work. Possible responses were "very satisfied," "somewhat satisfied," "somewhat dissatisfied," and "very dissatisfied."

Table 5-4 shows the proportions of women in each sample who reported dissatisfaction with each of these aspects of present life. Although the common-sense hypothesis would be that the widows' recent bereavement would create a sense of relative deprivation and dissatisfaction that would permeate many aspects of their lives, they are not uniformly less satisfied than the other women. The widows are clearly less satisfied than the other women on only three of these attributes, namely, family income, recreation, and the community of Kellogg generally. The survivors' wives are notably dissatisfied with their homes and furniture, and the other miners' wives are slightly more likely than the other women to say they are dissatisfied with their daily work.

Dissatisfaction with one of these attributes of life tends to be balanced with satisfaction with others, and therefore the average (mean) proportion of women reporting dissatisfaction varies little among samples, ranging from 24 percent for the widows to 22 percent for the survivors' wives and 20 percent for the other miners' wives. The widows are much more satisfied with their homes and furniture than are the other women, and there is no difference among samples in reported dissatisfaction with relationships to children.

The findings in table 5-4 suggest that the relationship between the general level of morale of widows or the other women and their satisfaction

Table 5-4

Reports of Dissatisfaction with Selected Aspects of Present Life
(percent)

	Percent Reporting That They Were "Somewhat Dissatisfied" or "Very Dissatisfied" about That Aspect of Their Present Life		
Measure of Satisfaction	*Widows*	*Survivors' Wives*	*Other Miners' Wives*
How do you feel about:			
1. Your family income	28	20	16
2. Your house and furniture	11	40	17
3. Your recreation	40	28	32
4. Your relationship with your children	6	8	5
5. The Kellogg community as a place in which to live	28	14	18
6. Your daily work	30	22	33

Number of cases were, respectively, 44, 50, and 128, except for the question about children, where they were 37, 48, and 123.

with these specific characteristics of their present situation is not very strong. Let us explore that suggestion more thoroughly by examining the statistical association between aspects of life satisfaction and reports of happiness.

This analysis involves sifting through a great deal of data, and to economize on space, the nature of the statistical tables presented will be altered somewhat. Instead of presenting extensive cross-tabulations in percentages, each cross-tabulation may be summarized in a single number, the correlation coefficient (r), and the table to be discussed will be a matrix of these coefficients. The larger the coefficient, the stronger the relationship between the variables in question. The relationship may be either positive, in which an increase in one variable is matched by a corresponding increase in the other, or negative, in which an increase in one is matched by a corresponding decrease in the other.

Normally the use of the correlation coefficient is limited to data that are in standard numerical or interval form rather than the "greater than" or "less than" nature, or *ordinal* scales, which we have used for many items in this study. The question on happiness, for example, with its response categories of "very happy," "relatively happy," and "not too happy," generates ordinal data, while the question on quality of life with its 10-point ladder scale generates interval data.

Some social scientists (see, for example, Labovitz 1970) have argued that the correlation coefficient may appropriately be used with ordinal data. In view of the greater interpretive power and economy of presentation inherent in its use, we shall take that position here. In other words, we shall relax the assumption of interval measurement and use the correlation coefficient as the measure of association for both interval and ordinal data. We have computed a more conventional measure of association (gamma) for the relationships that involve ordinal data, and the general patterns of association apparent in these gamma matrixes parallel those in the r matrixes presented in table 5-5.

The correlation coefficients in table 5-5 do not support the notion that dissatisfaction with these six aspects of life is any more a general characteristic of the widows than of the other women. If the coefficients in table 5-5 were all positive and statistically significant, it would mean that there was an underlying trait of general satisfaction or dissatisfaction with life that was reflected in similar scores on these separate items. If none of the coefficients were statistically significant and if there were about as many negative as positive ones, that would be evidence that the various dimensions of satisfaction were totally unrelated. What happens is this: the positive coefficients predominate but statistically significant relationships are few. Table 5-5 suggests that while there may be a general outlook of satisfaction or dissatisfaction that has some effect on the scores for the various aspects of life, the influence is not strong. The several dimensions

Table 5-5
Correlation Coefficients (*r*) among Selected Measures of Satisfaction with Life

Measure of Satisfaction	1	2	3	4	5	6
Widows						
1. Your family income	—	.05	− .03	− .35[a]	− .13	.27[a]
2. Your house and furniture		—	.11	.14	− .05	− .18
3. Your recreation			—	− .06	.10	.02
4. Your relationship with your children				—	.15	− .22
5. The Kellogg community as a place in which to live					—	− .06
6. Your daily work						—
Survivors' Wives						
1. Your family income	—	.55[a]	.25[a]	.01	.15	.11
2. Your house and furniture		—	.21	− .04	.22	− .05
3. Your recreation			—	.08	.11	.23
4. Your relationship with your children				—	.09	.16
5. The Kellogg community as a place in which to live					—	− .11
6. Your daily work						—
Other Miner's Wives						
1. Your family income	—	.28[a]	.15[a]	.08	.17[a]	.01
2. Your house and furniture		—	.24[a]	.23[a]	.07	− .03
3. Your recreation			—	.14	.14	.45[a]
4. Your relationship with your children				—	.31[a]	.10
5. The Kellogg community as a place in which to live					—	.31[a]
6. Your daily work						—

Note: Responses were scored from 1 (very satisfied) to 4 (very dissatisfied). Number of cases were, respectively, 44, 50 and 128, except for the question about children, where they were 37, 48, and 123.
[a]Statistically significant at the .05 level.

are distinctive enough that to view them as reflections of a general orientation of dissatisfaction would distort the more complex patterns that seem to exist, in which a woman states she is satisfied with one thing, partially satisfied with another, and dissatisfied with a third.

Judging from the number of statistically significant intercorrelations among these six measures of satisfaction, we conclude that there is more evidence for a general tendency toward dissatisfaction (or satisfaction) among the other miners' wives than either among the widows or the survivors' wives. The widows are noteworthy in that the expected positive relationship between satisfaction with family income and with recreation and house and furniture does not appear for them. The other miners' wives and survivors' wives who are satisfied with their family income also tend to be satisfied with their houses, furniture, and family recreation. The widows who are satisfied with family income, in contrast, are not necessarily happy with their homes or their recreational opportunities, and those widows who are satisfied with home and recreation are not always those satisfied with their income.

The widows are also unusual in that there are some negative correlations among the different dimensions of satisfaction. The largest of these is the cofficient of $-.35$ between satisfaction with family income and satisfaction with relationship to children. Because most women in all the samples report that they are satisfied with their relationships to their children, this finding may be interpreted to mean that the widows, those who are most satisfied with their ties to their children, are apt to be less satisfied with their family income. There are also negative coefficients between widows' satisfaction with work and satisfaction with children, house, and furniture. In other words, the widows who are dissatisfied with their daily work tend to be satisfied with their homes and their relationships to their children and vice versa.

In summary, the intercorrelations among reports of satisfaction with various aspect of life among widows are different from those for other women. Widows are more apt to exhibit incongruities or inconsistencies among the types of satisfaction. Rather than being characterized by a general outlook of either satisfaction or dissatisfaction, the widows manifest unusual discrepancies in level of perceived satisfaction. They are satisfied with some things but not others, while among the other women there is a modest trend toward congruity that produces positive correlation coefficients in almost every case. The appearance of greater discrepancies between the dimensions of satisfaction with life among the widows suggests that they are still in the process of reordering their lives. It may be anticipated that with time the discrepancies among the various types of life satisfaction will be reduced until as a group the widows manifest the same moderate level of congruity in life satisfaction as do in the other samples.

Happiness and Selected Measures of Satisfaction

Having examined the interconnections among measures of satisfaction, we will now consider how they relate to the women's reports of present happiness and quality of life. In part, this comparison may be seen as an attempt to validate our indices of happiness. If the single-item measures of happiness were positively related to the several life-satisfaction items, we could argue that the former were adequate reflections of life satisfaction generally or that a pervasive attitude of happiness underlies the responses about satisfaction with life. Furthermore, this comparison may permit the identification of important correlates of happiness. For example, it is easy to imagine situations in which some kinds of life satisfaction could be totally unrelated to a woman's perceptions of personal happiness. She might be highly satisfied with the kind of house she lived in but remain generally miserable because she hated her husband; or she might like the community but be unhappy because low family income forced her to live "across the tracks" rather than in a fine house on the hill.

The correlations between the 10-point estimation of present quality of life and 6 dimensions of satisfaction with life are presented in table 5-6. In all three samples the specific type of life satisfaction showing the strongest relationship to perceived quality of life is family income; second highest is the relationship between satisfaction with house and furniture and perceived quality of life. The widows are distinctive because none of the individual measures of life satisfaction is significantly related to quality of life. As in the previous table, there is evidence here that the widows' satisfaction with specific aspects of their lives is not linked very strongly to their overall feelings of happiness. More than the other women, widows are happy in some ways and unhappy in others; their general estimate of their own happiness is largely unrelated to their satisfaction with specific parts of their lives.

Table 5-7 presents a similar correlation matrix showing relationships between the three-point "very happy," "relatively happy," or "not too

Table 5-6
Correlation Coefficients (r) between Reports of Present Quality of Life and Selected Measures of Satisfaction with Life

Measure of Satisfaction	Widows	Survivors' Wives	Other Miners' Wives
1. Your family income	−.22	−.52[a]	−.29[a]
2. Your house and furniture	−.19	−.38[a]	−.20[a]
3. Your recreation	−.03	−.32[a]	−.18[a]
4. Your relationship with your children	−.09	−.15	−.07
5. The Kellogg community as a place in which to live	.12	−.29[a]	−.13
6. Your daily work	.10	−.26[a]	−.14

Note: The item on present quality of life is the "Where on the ladder do you feel you personally stand at the present time?" question discussed previously. Possible responses ranged from 1 to 10. Responses ranged from 1 (very satisfied) to 4 (very dissatisfied). Number of cases were, respectively, 44, 50, and 128, except for the question about children, where they were 37, 48, and 123.

[a]Statistically significant at the .05 level.

Table 5-7

Correlation Coefficients (*r*) between Reports of Happiness and Selected Measures of Satisfaction with Life

Measure of Satisfaction	Widows	Survivors' Wives	Other Miners' Wives
1. Your family income	.33[a]	.35[a]	.09
2. Your house and furniture	.04	.35[a]	.06
3. Your recreation	.02	.42[a]	.15[a]
4. Your relationship with your children	.10	.41[a]	.16[a]
5. The Kellogg community as a place in which to live	− .26[a]	.16	.19[a]
6. Your daily work	.06	.40[a]	.14

Note: The item on happiness used here was, "Taken all together, how would you say things are these days—would you say that you are very happy, relatively happy, or not too happy?" Responses were scored ranging from 1 (very happy) to 3 (not too happy). Responses ranged from 1 (very satisfied) to 4 (very dissatisfied). Number of cases were, respectively, 43, 50, and 128, except for the question about children, where they were 36, 48, and 123.
[a]Statistically significant at the .05 level.

happy" questions and six items on life satisfaction. These findings generally parallel those in table 5-6. For the survivors' wives and the other miners' wives, the global measure of happiness is positively related to the specific types of satisfaction, usually significantly so, but it is not true for the widows. However, there are two exceptions to this pattern: widows' satisfaction with family income is related to their perceptions of being happy, and their statements about the Kellogg community as a place to live are negatively related to their reports of happiness. In other words, the widows who say that Kellogg is a good place to live tend to be those who say their present lives are unhappy, and those who dislike the community tend to say that they are relatively happy.

Perhaps the most useful finding in tables 5-6 and 5-7 is the additional evidence for widows that satisfaction with family income is a stronger correlate of personal happiness than any of the other five measures of life satisfaction. A link between money and happiness is found in all the samples, but it is more noticeable among the widows because for them satisfaction with other aspects of life is not strongly related to happiness.

Self-Esteem

One adaptation to sudden losses and wrenched relationships of widowhood is self-depreciation. Suttee, the East Indian practice of the widow throwing herself upon her husband's funeral pyre, has no official counterpart in modern western society, but its psychological equivalents are quite common. It is not a widow's fault that her husband has died, and yet she often finds herself treated as if it were. "The prevailing attitudes force a widow to feel like a displaced person. She has been tainted by the unmentionable. She is a leper, an outcast, a pariah" (Lewis 1975:6).

The work from which these dramatic pronouncements are taken claims in its dedication to be based on interviews with 325 widows "who sat down with us to tell it like it is," but the only evidence presented in the book is drawn from case histories or illustrative examples. The reader is never told how many of the 325 widows suffer from low self-esteem, how many feel like displaced persons, or how their feelings of rejection compare to those of nonwidows. Nevertheless, there seems ample justification for viewing the status of widowhood as stigmatizing and isolating:

> "Hot potato," "third eye," "fifth wheel," "hole in the head," "sinking ship," "ice in winter," "broken arm,"—widows had many unflattering terms to describe how their married friends had made them feel. To a greater or lesser degree, there was a sameness to the pattern of what they had all experienced. With their husbands, they had been part of a couple-oriented soc al circle. There was no room in it for a single woman and, when they were widowed and became that, the circle closed, leaving them on the outside. (Lewis 1975:74)

This psychological and social stigmatization is presumed to have a negative impact on the self-concept of the widow. We would expect the Sunshine Mine widows to illustrate the results of this stigmatization by having lower self-esteem than the other women. Interviewed six months after widowhood, they had had a chance to see their old friendship networks deteriorate. In addition, they have experienced an identity crisis with all the self-doubts and fears that accompany such crises at any period of life. Plainly their self-images should be less healthy than those of other women in the community.

There is little evidence in the responses to questions on attitude toward the self that the widows are very different from the other women. In their responses to a standard 10-item scale designed to measure self-esteem (Rosenberg 1963), widows do not appear to suffer from low self-esteem. The items are presented in table 5-8 along with the proportions of women giving the low self-esteem answer in each case. The notable finding in the table is that the widows and the survivors' wives manifest no differences in self-esteem. In only one of the ten items, "I feel that I have a number of good qualities," is there a difference between the two groups of more than 10 percent. In fact, there were only four of the ten items in which more than 10 percentage points separated any of the groups, and on two of these four it was the survivors' wives rather than the widows who were most different from the other miners' wives. On those items where the greatest intersample differences appeared, it was the other miners' wives rather than the widows who manifested the lower self-esteem.

Table 5-8
Percentage of Women Giving the "Low" Self-Esteem Response on Ten Items about the Self

Item	Widows	Survivors' Wives	Other Miners' Wives
All in all, I am inclined to feel that I am a failure. (Agree.)	5	2	4
I feel I do not have much to be proud of. (Agree.)	9	8	2
I wish I could have more respect for myself. (Agree.)	25	16	20
I am able to do things as well as most other people. (Disagree.)	47	42	67
At times I think I am no good at all. (Agree.)	48	42	42
I feel that I am a person of worth, at least on an equal plane with others. (Disagree.)	48	48	63
I take a positive attitude toward myself. (Disagree.)	49	54	63
I feel that I have a number of good qualities. (Disagree.)	50	38	64
On the whole, I am satisified with myself. (Disagree.)	57	54	58
I certainly feel useless at times. (Agree.)	66	58	68
(N)	(44)	(50)	(128)

[a]May vary slightly due to nonresponse or "do not know" response.

The use of the comparison samples has demonstrated that some of the existing stereotypes about widows may not be completely true. Of course, widows can be found whose personal statements illustrate low self-esteem, but such women are also found among the nonwidows. To the degree that writings on widowhood use impressionistic evidence from a few widows to document the point that they suffer from low self-esteem without gathering comparable evidence from the nonwidowed, the inaccurate stereotypes will be perpetuated.

Summary

We make no claim that the present findings are definitive. The Sunshine Mine widows are unusual in many ways, and generalization to other widows and situations must be tentative. The evidence presented in this chapter suggests that by six months after widowhood, these widows were experiencing positive feelings in the usual frequency. They were still prey to many more negative feelings, however, especially loneliness, restlessness, boredom, and depression, than were women in the comparison samples. Despite this overabundance of negative feelings, many of the widows had adopted a lifestyle that they could describe as happy, their aspirations for the future were normal, and they were not notably lacking in self-esteem. Perhaps the most atypical thing about them is their redefinition of the past in rosier terms than can reasonably be accepted. The widows are also distinctive because their attitudes about specific characteristics of their present life are inconsistent. More than the other women, they were happy in some ways but not in others. Although they are more apt to feel restless, lonely, and depressed than other women, the linkage between these negative feelings and the self-concept has not been demonstrated to be very strong. Most of them are lonely and restless, but there is little evidence that they suffer from low self-esteem. The future looks good to them, as good as it does to those who are not bereaved.

References

Barrett, Carol. J. 1977. "Women in Widowhood." *Signs* 2 (Summer):856-868.

Bowlby, John. 1960. "Grief and Mourning in Early Infancy and Childhood." *The Psychoanalytic Study of the Child* 15:9-20.

_____. 1969. *Attachment and Loss, Vol. 1, Attachment.* New York: Basic Books.

_____. 1973. *Attachment and Loss, Vol. 2, Separation, Anxiety and Anger.* New York: Basic Books.

Bradburn, Norman M. 1969. *The Structure of Psychological Well-Being.* Chicago: Aldine.

Caine, Lynn. 1974. *Widow.* New York: Morrow.

Cantril, Hadley. 1966. *The Pattern of Human Concerns.* New Brunswick, New Jersey: Rutgers University Press.

Carey, Raymond G. 1977. "The Widowed: A Year Later." *Journal of Counseling Psychology* 24 (no. 2):125-131.

Condie, Spencer J., and Doan, Han T. 1978. "Role Profit and Marital Satisfaction Throughout the Family Life Cycle." *Journal of Comparative Family Studies* 9 (June):257-267.

Eliot, Thomas B. 1930a. "The Adjusted Behavior of Bereaved Families: A New Field of Research." *Social Forces* 8 (June):543-549.

_____. 1930b. "Bereavement as a Problem for Family Research and Technique." *The Family* 11 (June):114-115.

_____. 1932. "The Bereaved Family." *Annals of the American Academy of Political and Social Science* 160:184-190.

Freud, Sigmund. 1917. "Mourning and Melancholia." In *Collected Papers*, vol. 4, pp. 152-170. New York: Basic Books, 1959.

Fulconer, David M. 1942. "The Adjustive Behavior of Some Recently Bereaved Spouses: A Psycho-Sociological Study." Unpublished doctoral dissertation, Northwestern University.

Gurin, G., Veroff, J., and Feld, S. 1960. *Americans View Their Mental Health*. New York: Basic Books.

Harvey, Carol D., and Bahr, Howard M. 1974. "Widowhood, Morale, and Affiliation." *Journal of Marriage and the Family*, 36 (February):97-106.

Labovitz, Sanford, 1970. "The Assignment of Numbers to Rank Order Categories." *American Sociological Review* 35 (June):515-524.

Lewis, Alfred Allan. 1975. *Three Out of Four Wives*. New York: Macmillan.

Nye, F. Ivan, and Berardo, Felix M. 1973. *The Family: Its Structure and Interaction*. New York: Macmillan.

Rodgers, Willard I., and Converse, Philip E. 1975. "Measures of the Perceived Overall Quality of Life." *Social Indicators Research* 2:127-152.

Rosenberg, Morris. 1963. "Parental Interest and Children's Self-Conceptions." *Sociometry* 26 (March):35-49.

Switzer, David K. 1970. *The Dynamics of Grief*. Nashville, Tenn.: Abingdon Press.

6 Correlates of Morale

In chapter 5 we noted that the widows' attitudes of personal unhappiness and worry reflected their bereavement. It is noteworthy that some of them did not worry more now than formerly and many of them still seemed to be happy. In this chapter we will discover what distinguishes those widows whose responses do not reflect serious loss of morale or difficulty in adjustment to their new status from their less fortunate peers.

Our identification of women's characteristics that may facilitate adjustment to widowhood will involve an examination of the relationship between reports of present happiness or high quality of life and several indicators of the women's personal characteristics and social participation. It will proceed in four stages. First, we examine the relationship between certain demographic characteristics (age, education, income, and whether or not she had been married previously) and happiness. Next, aspects of social involvement are considered, including activity in voluntary organizations and during leisure time and contacts with relatives and friends. Third, the linkage between religiosity and happiness is explored. Finally, we will compare the relative strengths of social activities and person characteristics when considered in combination as antecedents of happiness.

The Impact of Personal Characteristics

Among the factors that have been shown to affect widows' morale are personal characteristics and patterns of involvement with kin, friends, and social or religious organizations. Older and better educated widows are said to show better adjustment (Carey 1977) as are the upper-income widows (Harvey and Bahr 1974). Extent of social participation and contact with others is highly related to morale (Arling 1976; Atchley 1975; Lopata 1970; Walker, MacBride, and Vachon, 1977). For many of the newly widowed, religious beliefs and activity also sustain morale and are a major source of comfort (Glick, Weiss, and Parkes 1974:133-134).

The question of whether a widow's age, education, income, or former marital status is related to the level of happiness she reports might be answered without referring to the data from the survivors' or other miners' wives. Having noted how these factors seem to influence a widow's happiness, it will be instructive to learn if their effects seem to follow the same pattern for women who are not widows. In other words, do the characteristics that seem related to personal happiness among the widows influence other women in the same direction? Is there something about the status of widow that brings certain characteristics to the fore or that minimizes the influence of attributes that in more normal circumstances are related to personal happiness?

Table 6-1 contains correlation coefficients showing the strength of the associations between the characteristics of the women and reports of unhappiness and of quality of life. The most interesting findings illustrate the "buffering" effects of certain characteristics upon the widows' happiness. For example, the older widows were more likely to report unhappiness than were younger ones, but there is no relationship between age and unhappiness in other samples. Education seems to exert an even stronger influence on widows' happiness but to have little bearing on the happiness or perceived life quality of the other women. Current family income makes a difference in either unhappiness or perceived life quality for all three samples, and the difference is consistently as we would predict. Higher income people have higher life quality and more happiness than lower income people.

The fourth row of table 6-1 contains only one significant coefficient, the r of $-.28$ for the association between a previous marriage and present unhappiness. For the widows who had been previously divorced and remarried before losing a husband in the Sunshine fire, the impact of the loss on morale seems to be greater than for the other widows.

The major conclusion to be drawn from table 6-1 is that certain characteristics that are not related to happiness or life quality among women generally seem to have special salience for widows. Age, education, and the marital status of "remarried" are examples of those characteristics. Other attributes such as family income have a consistent bearing on morale whether one is widowed or happily married.

One of the problems in using the correlation coefficient to signal meaningful relationships is that its use assumes the existence of linear or straight-line relationships. In a linear relationship an increase in one variable A is presumed to be matched by changes in the other variable B. Incremental increases in A are also matched to the same order increments in B. If a relationship between two variables is curvilinear, the correlation coefficient may not represent the nature of the association adequately because it reflects an averaging of the relation between income and happiness at all levels of both. For example, if wives in both low-income and high-income families are unhappy while wives in middle-income families are happy, then an analyst might conclude from a low correlation coefficient that income and happiness were not related. In fact, receiving family incomes that were at either extreme of the continuum would be linked to unhappiness. The correlation coefficient may not be effective in the search for relationships more complex than the simple linear model.

Table 6-1
Correlation Coefficients (r) between Unhappiness, Quality of Life, and Selected Demographic Characteristics of the Women

Selected Characteristics	Unhappiness			Quality of Life		
	Widows	Survivors' Wives	Other Miners' Wives	Widows	Survivors' Wives	Other Miners' Wives
Age	.49[a]	.05	.09	-.13	.22	.05
Education	-.52[a]	-.14	-.10	.53[a]	.17	.06
Family income (1972)	-.16	-.08	-.19[a]	.33[a]	.32[a]	.11
Married before	-.28[a]	.12	-.08	.06	-.09	.05
(N)	(44)	(50)	(128)	(44)	(50)	(128)

Note: The characteristics were defined as follows: Age was scored 1 to 11, in the following categories: under 20, 20-24, 25-29, 30-34, 35-39, 40-44, 45-49, 50-54, 55-59, 60-64, 65 and over; education was scored 1 to 8, with the categories of no schooling, some grade school, completed grade school, technical specialty, some high school, high school graduate, some college, and college graduate; 1972 family income was scored in 10 categories: $1,000-$2,999, $3,000-$4,999, $5,000-$6,999, $7,000-$8,999, $9,000-$10,999, $11,000-$12,999, $13,000-$14,999, $15,000-$16,999, $17,000-$18,999, and $19,000 and over; the responses to the "Were you ever married before?" question were coded for this analysis as interval "dummy variables" (all or nothing categories) with 0 denoting a previous marriage and 1 standing for the present (or, for widows, the recent) marriage being the first. "Unhappiness" scores ranged from 1 ("very happy") to 3 ("not too happy"). The item on present quality of life is the "Where on the ladder do you feel you personally stand at the present time?" question discussed previously. Possible responses ranged from 1 to 10. Number of cases varied slightly, usually by only a single case; these are the modal Ns.

[a]Statistically significant at the .05 level.

To clarify how "buffer" variables affect perceived happiness or quality of life, the samples were subdivided into somewhat homogeneous categories with respect to age, education, and family income. For each category the proportion of women claiming a "high" quality of present life was computed and charted as shown in the profiles, figures 6-1 and 6-2. The decision about what scores represent a "high" quality of life was made with reference to the distribution of responses in each sample. We divided each distribution into two categories of roughly equal size. Half the widows chose a number between 6 and 10 in estimating their quality of present life on the 10-point scale, and thus the cutting point for them was set at step 6. Widows who chose numbers between 6 and 10 were then defined as having "high quality" or "happy" lives. The distribution of scores for the other women was generally higher than for the widows; in other words, the average survivors' and other miners' wife chose a quality-of-life score more than halfway up the ladder. Fifty-two percent of the former and 69 percent of the latter selected scores of 7 or higher on the 10-point scale. For these two groups, accordingly, a "high quality" life was defined as one designated by a score of 7 or greater, in contrast to 6 or greater for widows.

Now examine the reports of high quality of life (also referred hereafter as "happiness") among women in the different age groups as shown in figure 6-1. Among widows the pattern is fairly consistent, with only a slight reversal in the oldest age group (women 50 and over): The older widows are less happy than the younger ones. It should be remembered that our entire sample of widows is younger than many widowed populations. Apparently among a fairly young widowed group, the younger ones have an easier time of it than the middle-aged. Beyond a certain point, presumably at an age when widowhood is no longer so atypical, the pattern begins to reverse itself.

We see a curvilinear pattern in figure 6-1 among the survivors' wives, which is masked in the positive correlation coefficient between age and quality of life that appears in table 6-1. The profile reveals that among survivors' wives under age 50, the older women report higher levels of happiness than the younger women. It is only in the group aged 50 and over that reported levels of happiness drop, and even then they are not as low as they are among the survivors' wives under age 30. The contrast between the profiles for the widows and the survivors' wives suggests that we need to beware of superficial generalizations about the effects of age on perceived happiness.

Finally, if we examined only the profile of the other miners' wives, we might conclude that age has very little to do with perceptions of happiness. There is a gentle downward slope of the profile until its increase among the oldest women is congruent with but not as marked as the pattern for widows.

The effects of education seem less complex. Among the widows and survivors' wives, a linear pattern does emerge with more reported happiness for each higher level of education. Among the other miners' wives, the pro-

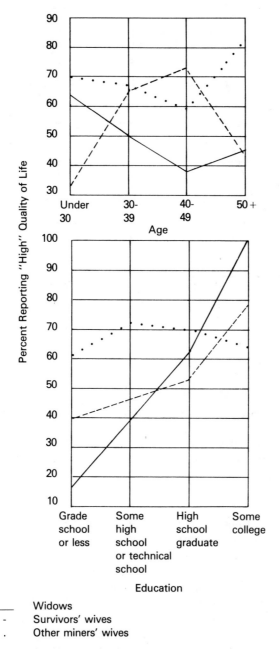

Note: A "high" quality of life was defined as 6-10 on the 10-point scale for widows, 7-10 for women in the other samples.

Figure 6-1. Percent of Women Reporting a High Present Quality of Life, by Age and Education

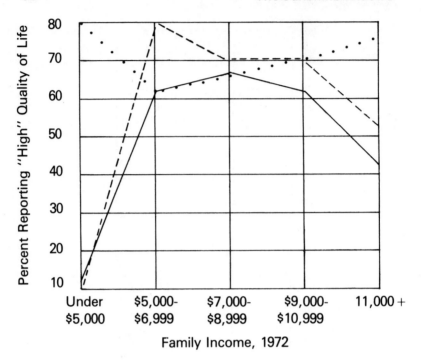

Family Income, 1972

_____ Widows
- - - - Survivors' wives
. . . . Other miners' wives

A "high" quality of life was defined as 6-10 on the 10-point scale for widows, 7-10 for women
in the other samples.

Figure 6-2. Percent of Women Reporting a High Present Quality of Life,
by Present Family Income and Activity in Voluntary Organizations

file shows little relationship between happiness and educational attainment
contrary to the expected pattern.

Figure 6-2 contains evidence that some other curvilinear relationships
were masked in the correlational analysis in table 6-1. Note the linkage between family income and quality of life. Among both the widows and the
survivors' wives, the lowest income category includes very few happy
women. There is a sharp increase in reported happiness in the three middle-
income categories, with women in families having annual incomes of between $5,000 and $7,000 per year reporting about the same level of happiness as women in families reporting incomes of between $9,000 and
$11,000 per year. Among the women reporting the highest family incomes,

in excess of $11,000 per year, the rate of reported happiness drops. In this high-income category, between 45 and 55 percent of the women in these two samples report a high quality of life, compared to between 60 and 70 percent in the two next-lower income categories.

Once again the profile for the other miners' wives is atypical, with a consistent but very modest trend of increases in the rate of reported happiness as family income increases. Little should be made of the high rate of reported happiness among the other miners' wives in the lowest income category because it is based on a small subsample of five cases.

Happiness and Social Involvement

Our exploration of the relationship between social activity and happiness will include contacts with relatives and friends, participation in voluntary organizations, leisure activity, and vicarious social activity via the mass media.

Let us first look at the effects of varying rates of interaction with friends and relatives. Table 6-2 presents the correlation coefficients between five measures of interaction with friends and relatives and the women's perceptions of their happiness and quality of life. The consistently low coefficients suggest that number of contacts with friends and relatives has little to do with happiness or perceived quality of life. Women who write letters or visit relatives do not seem any happier than those who do not.

The basic finding that perceptions of happiness among these women seem unrelated to their having close friends in the community is also supported by the results in table 6-3. In fact, the most sizable difference in the table indicates that widows who had close friends among the wives of non-miners are considerably *less* likely to presently consider themselves happy than are those who did not have friends outside the network of miners. For friends among the wives of other miners in the community, the direction of the relationship is the same: widows who claim close friends at the time of the fire are less likely to consider themselves happy than are those who did not have close friends before the disaster.

The happier widows are those who report a change in friends since bereavement. Presumably the pattern that appears in rows 5 and 6 of table 6-3 is a consequence of the widows' changed marital status and accompanying change in the functions of friendship. For example, old friendships based on "coupleness" might prove difficult to maintain for a women suddenly alone. Single women, divorcees, or other widows who had been acquaintances might become more important as confidants or close friends for an insecure widow unexpectedly facing single life once more.

Existing research suggests a positive link between involvement in com-

Table 6-2
Correlation Coefficients (r) between Unhappiness, Quality of Life, and Contact with Relatives and Friends

Measure of Contact	Unhappiness			Quality of Life		
	Widows	Survivors' Wives	Other Miners' Wives	Widows	Survivors' Wives	Other Miners' Wives
During the past week, how many times did you:						
Visit relatives	.01	.29[b]	-.07	-.05	-.01	.03
Visit friends	-.01	-.09	-.10	.08	.03	.11
Telephone relatives	-.12	.24	.02	.20	.03	-.10
Telephone friends	-.01	.10	-.22[b]	.00	-.03	.27[b]
Write a personal letter	.05	.06	.14	.11	.08	.11
(N)[a]	(43)	(50)	(128)	(44)	(50)	(128)

Note: All of these measures of contacts were scored on a 5-point scale with 1 = 1-2 reported contacts (visits, telephone calls, or letters); 2 = 3-4; 3 = 5-6; 4 = 7-8; and 5 = 9 or more contacts. Scores ranged from 1 ("very happy") to 3 ("not too happy"). The item on present quality of life is the question, "Where on the ladder do you feel you personally stand at the present time?" discussed previously. Possible responses ranged from 1 to 10.

[a]Number of cases varied slightly, usually by only a single case; these are the modal Ns.
[b]Statistically significant at the .05 level.

Table 6-3

Proportions of Women Indicating that They Are "Very Happy" by Presence of Close Friends and Change in Friendship Network

Friendship Characteristic	Percent "Very Happy"		
	Widows	Survivors' Wives	Other Miners' Wives
	% (N)	% (N)	% (N)
Some people have close friends to whom they can confide their worries, hopes, dreams, and problems. Did you have close friends of this type who were the wives of miners before the fire?			
Yes	40 (20)	40 (30)	35 (88)
No	50 (22)	45 (20)	32 (40)
Before the disaster, did you have close friends of this type who were the wives of men in other occupations?			
Yes	38 (29)	42 (38)	37 (94)
No	62 (13)	42 (12)	26 (34)
Since the mine disaster, has your group of friends changed?			
Yes	57 (21)	29 (14)	37 (19)
No	32 (22)	47 (36)	34 (108)

Note: For the widows, both "very happy" and "relatively happy" are included in the "high happiness" category; for survivors' and other miners' wives, "very happy" only. Also note that the N figure is the percentage base, not the number of cases reported in the percentage to the left. The 40 percent in row 1, column 1, should be interpreted as follows: Of the 20 widows who said that they had close friends who were miners' wives, 40 percent rated themselves as "very happy" or "relatively happy."

munity organizations and widows' morale. Lopata has suggested, "Voluntary associations may provide greater emotional satisfaction to the widow as sources of continued contact and identification with people defined as similar" (Lopata 1970:54). We reasoned a similar connection should exist between time spent in leisure-time activities and morale. Women who fill their time with specific activities were expected to have higher morale than women who were not involved in such pursuits.

The items on participation in voluntary organizations asked specifically whether the respondents belonged to seven types of organizations, including fellowship organizations, labor unions or professional groups, political or action organizations, recreational or social groups, hobby groups, community or neighborhood organizations, and a residual category of "any other type of organization." A rough measure of the scope or diversity of a woman's organizational affiliations was obtained by counting the number of the types of affiliation she maintained. An estimate of the extent of her organizational activity was then obtained via the question, "In the last month how many meetings did you go to including committee meetings?''

An item on leisure activities followed questions about reading and television viewing and asked, "What other types of leisure activities occupy your time most? For example, do you sew, bake, fish, hike, or do any other leisure activities?" A single item quantifying extent of leisure activity followed, saying, "Approximately how much time did you spend in other leisure activities yesterday, besides TV and reading?"

The correlation coefficients among the indicators of social activity and the women's perceptions of happiness and life quality appear in table 6-4. Among the widows, the number of meetings attended and the diversity of organizational affiliations are related to happiness as expected. Hours of leisure activity seem to have little levels of happiness for any of our samples. It should also be stressed that the positive relationship between happiness and both meeting attendance and diversity of affiliation among the widows does not appear for the survivors' wives and other miners' wives. The notion that the affiliative ties bound the widows who had them to meaningful social groups and thereby increased their morale is thus supported by our results.

The relationship between activity in organizations and life quality may be assessed in greater depth by examining the profiles in figure 6-3. Note that among the survivors' and other miners' wives, women with no organizational involvement report lower levels of happiness than women with a moderate amount of such activity. The women who are the most active in organizations are no more likely to report high levels of personal happiness than are those with no activity at all. The pattern for widows does not entirely conform to this generalization, however. Widows with no organizational activity are least likely to report personal happiness, and as extent of activity increases, the level of reported happiness increases as well. The widows who report the most activity (9 or more meetings per month) are no more happy than those who report modest activity (3-8 meetings per month). Although on the face of it these profiles support the conclusion that activity in community organizations is related to widows' happiness, it should be remembered that there was a strong inverse relationship between widows' education and reported happiness ($r = -.53$), and there is some evidence that it is the more educated widows who are most active in community organizations ($r = .33$) to about the same degree that activity in organizations is associated with high quality of life ($r = .31$).

Effects of Religiosity and Church Attendance

Do religious belief and activity foster higher morale among widows? The evidence for this question, while unsystematic and tentative, seems to point to a positive influence of religiosity. Many widows claim that their religious

Table 6-4
Correlation Coefficients (r) between Unhappiness, Quality of Life, and Selected Measures of Social Activity

Measure of Social Activity	Unhappiness			Quality of Life		
	Widows	Survivors' Wives	Other Miners' Wives	Widows	Survivors' Wives	Other Miners' Wives
Number of organization meetings attended in the past month	−.08	.06	−.04	.31[a]	.17	−.01
Diversity of organizational affiliations[a]	−.29[c]	.08	−.13	.27[c]	.16	.07
Hours spend in "other leisure activities" yesterday	.21	−.08	−.14	.02	.22	.12
(N)[b]	(42)	(50)	(128)	(42)	(50)	(128)

Note: Scores for meeting attendance were $0 = 0$, $1\text{-}2 = 1$, $3\text{-}4 = 2$, $5\text{-}6 = 3$, $7\text{-}8 = 4$, and $9+ = 5$. Diversity of organizational affiliation scores ranged from 0 to 5, although the possible range went up to 7. Scores ranged from 1 ("very happy") to 3 ("not too happy"). The item on present quality of life is the question, "Where on the ladder do you feel you personally stand at the present time?" discussed previously. Possible responses ranged from 1 to 10.

[a]Number of types of organizations, out of the eight possible categories, ranged from 0 (no affiliations) to 5.
[b]Number of cases varied slightly, usually by only a single case; these are the modal Ns.
[c]Statistically significant at the .05 level.

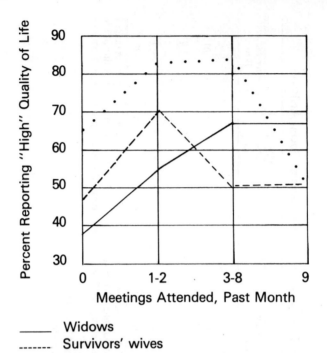

Widows
------- Survivors' wives
. . . . Other miners' wives

Note: A "high" quality of life was defined as 6-10 on the 10-point scale for widows, 7-10 for women in the other samples.

Figure 6-3. Percent of Women Reporting a High Present Quality of Life, by Activity in Voluntary Organizations

beliefs help them to cope with bereavement (Barrett 1977:867; Glick, Weiss, and Parkes 1974:133-134), and there is also a connection between church activity and the maintenance of other forms of social involvement. Lopata (1970:54) writes that "the older widow depends mainly upon her 'religion' for comfort and support . . ." (1970:54) and that "memberships of older widows are so often connected with a church" (1973:250). Provided that these findings may be generalized to younger widows, it follows that religious belief and activity should be positively related to widows' perceptions of happiness and quality of life. That hypothesis may be tested with the data in table 6-5, which shows the proportions of women by category of church membership, belief, or participation, who indicated that they had a very happy life or gave a high quality of life score. The general conclusion to be drawn is that among widows church membership and participation are positively related to happiness. For example, widows who said they were

Table 6-5

Percent of Women Reporting That They Are "Very Happy" or Having a "High Quality" Life, by Selected Indicators of Religiosity and Church Attendance

Indicator of Religiosity or Church Participation	Percent "Very Happy" or with "High" Life Quality		
	Widows % (N)	Survivors' Wives % (N)	Other Miners' Wives % (N)
Membership			
Members	52 (27)	33 (21)	39 (79)
Nonmembers	31 (16)	48 (29)	26 (49)
Salience			
The "very religious"	62 (13)	44 (9)	37 (30)
Others	38 (29)	41 (41)	34 (98)
Attendance			
Weekly or "nearly every week"	53 (19)	33 (15)	41 (51)
Others	38 (24)	49 (35)	30 (77)
Participates in social events			
Yes	69 (16)	20 (10)	32 (38)
No	30 (27)	52 (33)	35 (85)
Changes in religiosity since disaster			
Increased	55 (22)	48 (21)	35 (43)
Same	29 (14)	35 (26)	32 (81)
Decreased	43 (7)	50 (2)	100 (1)
Percent Reporting "High" Quality of Life Church Activity or Membership Widows			
Membership			
Members	52 (27)	62 (21)	72 (79)
Nonmembers	47 (17)	48 (29)	63 (49)
Salience			
The "very religious"	62 (13)	78 (9)	83 (30)
Others	43 (30)	49 (41)	64 (98)
Attendance			
Weekly or "nearly every week"	53 (19)	53 (15)	75 (51)
Others	48 (25)	54 (35)	65 (77)
Participates in social events			
Yes	75 (16)	60 (10)	68 (38)
No	36 (28)	58 (33)	68 (85)
Increased religiosity since disaster			
Increased	57 (23)	52 (21)	63 (43)
Same	43 (14)	58 (26)	70 (81)
Decreased	43 (7)	50 (2)	100 (1)

Note: For the widows, both "very happy" and "relatively happy" are included in the "high happiness" category; for survivors' and other miners' wives, "very happy" only. "High" quality of life was defined as 6-10 for widows, 7-10 for the other samples. Note also that N this is the percentage base, not the number of cases represented in the percentage at the left. The 52 percent in row 1, column 1 should be interpreted as follows: "of the 27 widows who said they were church members, 52 percent rated themselves as "very happy" or "relatively happy."

"very religious" were twice as apt as the other women to say they were "happy" or "very happy," and those who said they participated in church social activities were more than twice as likely as the others to say they were happy or to pick a "high" life-quality score for their life at the time of the interview. In all three samples, where there is a difference in morale between the religious and the nonreligious, it is the religious who are happier or who have higher quality of life scores. Among the other miners' wives and sometimes for the survivors' wives, however, the religious variables often have little influence one way or the other upon morale. Apparently religious activity and belief, like education, are attributes that are more directly related to high morale among widows than in the general population.

Comparing the Relative Influence of Correlates of Happiness

Having considered widows' personal characteristics, contact with friends and relatives, and religiosity as possible correlates of happiness, we may now compare their individual and combined effects. The effects of 15 independent variables will be considered. All but one of these are variables discussed previously in this chapter. They include four personal demographic characteristics, the respondent's age, education, family income (1972), and whether or not she had been married before. Inasmuch as perceived or relative income (what one earns in comparison to what relatives and friends earn) may be as important as absolute income, the attitudinal variable "satisfaction with income" was added as a personal characteristic. There are then six items on the extent of the social network; two are about voluntary associations (number of meetings attended in the past month and the measure of diversity of organizational affiliation introduced earlier in this chapter); one is a summary measure of contact with friends and relatives introduced in chapter 4; two measures are of friendship ties at the time of the fire, one pertaining to the presence of close friends in the community and the other to participation in social activities; and there is an item on hours of leisure activity on the day preceding the interview. Finally, there are four items on religious involvement including church membership, church attendance, how religious the respondent thought herself, and whether or not she participated in church social activities.

To estimate the relative strength of these 15 variables upon perceptions of happiness, we performed a stepwise multiple-regression analysis. In effect, multiple-regression analysis permits several independent variables to compete with each other to determine which has the strongest individual relationship to the dependent variable. In addition, it provides an overall summary measure of how much of the variation in the dependent variable can be explained by various combinations of the independent variables. The stepwise regression technique begins with the one variable having the highest correlation with the dependent variable, then having allowed for that fraction of the total variation which that first independent variable explains, adds the independent variable that explains the next highest amount of variation in the dependent variable, and so on. This process continues until the addition of new variables has no significant effect on the dependent variable.

The stepwise regression technique permits us to take the 15 independent variables and assess which of them has any important effect on the women's perceptions of happiness and quality of life after the other more powerful variables have been taken into account. At the same time it provides an estimate of how much of the differences in women's happiness of life quality may be accounted for by the combination of variables identified as "significant" influences.

It is recognized that regression analysis assumes measurement on interval scales and that most of our variables were measured on ordinal scales. There is literature justifying the use of interval statistics with ordinal data (Labovitz 1967, 1970, 1971; Borgatta 1968), and it seems to be an appropriate way to obtain rough estimates of the relative impact of the various possible predictors of widows' morale.

The detailed results from the analysis of the effects of the 15 independent variables on perceptions of unhappiness and quality of life will be published elsewhere (Bahr and Harvey 1980) and will not be presented here. We will summarize the major findings, as follows. First, usually only three or four of the 15 variables had a significant influence on variations in happiness or quality of life. Second, a combination of 3 or 4 independent variables were able to explain much of the variation in happiness or life quality for the widows. In contrast, for the survivors' and other miners' wives none of the possible combinations of the 15 variables explained very much of the intrasample differences in happiness. Specifically, for the widows only 3 variables—education, age, and religiosity, in that order—combined to account for almost half of the total explained variance in happiness. In the other samples level of explained variation in perceived happiness ranged from 24 percent (survivors' wives) to only 9 percent (other miners' wives).

Third, the results of the stepwise regression analysis revealed that the factors associated with high morale among widows were not the best predictors of morale for women in the comparison samples. For the widows, being happy was strongly affected by being young, being relatively well educated, and feeling that one was a religious person, and having a high quality of life was most dependent on education and family income. In contrast, income, satisfaction with income, and being socially active were the key predictors of morale for the other women. Once again relative youth and educational attainment have appeared as significant "buffer variables" associated with successful adaptation to sudden widowhood.

An Alternative Measure of Adjustment to Widowhood

We have used widows' statements about their happiness at the time of the interview to estimate their adjustment to widowhood. An alternative approach that takes into account each woman's perception of both past and present life quality may provide a more meaningful indication of adjustment. The utility of comments about a given level of life quality is greatly enhanced when they may be compared to a former, or even a future situation. For example, some people may consistently define their life situation in negative terms, and a statement to an interviewer to that effect would merely indicate stability of life situation rather than poor adjustment; however, without estimates of former life quality, the interviewer would have no way of knowing that a given "negative" score represented a pessimistic outlook or continuing negative situation.

The items on perceptions of life quality five years before, when considered along with the women's estimates of present life quality, permit a kind of "self-anchoring" of the life-quality scales. For all three samples we can compare present estimates of life quality to estimates for five years ago. The numerical answers to this question appear in table 6-6. Thirty-five percent of the other miners' wives and 30 percent of the survivors' wives had a net improvement of life quality of three or more points (on the 1 to 10 scale) over the past five years. The comparable figure for the widows was 9 percent. Although many of the women in the comparison samples defined the present as significantly better than the past, the most frequent responses were in the range of relative stability of life quality. The score given at the time of the interview was within two points of the score estimated for five years ago. Sixty-two percent of the survivors' wives exhibited such relative stability compared to 41 percent of the widows. The average net change scores were 1.52 and 2.10 for the survivors' and other miners' wives, compared to a mean decline of -2.36 for the widows.

To recapitulate; the great majority of women in the two comparison samples reported quality of life scores for the present and five-year-ago past such that their quality of life had either remained stable or improved. About two thirds of them had present quality of life scores within a point or two of the scores for five years ago. In contrast, half of the widows perceived losses in quality of life scores of three or more points, and only 9 percent reported a definite (three or more points) improvement.

In view of their recent bereavement, for some Sunshine widows to maintain that their life quality was relatively the same as it used to be may be in-

Table 6-6
Five-Year Change in Perceived Quality of Life, Present Compared to Five Years Ago

Nature of Change	Extent of Change	Widows (%)	Survivors' Wives (%)	Other Miners' Wives (%)
Improvement	9	—	—	2
	8	2	—	2
	7	—	2	2
	6	—	2	6
	5	—	4	6
	4	2	12	10
	3	5	10	7
Relative stability	2	9	24	21
	1	7	10	11
	0	5	22	23
	−1	9	2	3
	−2	11	10	4
Decline	−3	9	—	2
	−4	7	2	—
	−5	16	—	1
	−6	9	—	—
	−7			
	−8			
	−9			
(N)		(44)	(50)	(127)

terpreted as evidence of successful adjustment to widowhood. In these terms precisely half the widows had made a successful adjustment.

Correlates of Adjustment

We have said that half the widows had made a positive adjustment to widowhood in that their numerical estimates of present quality of life were about the same as for five years ago. To identify the women's characteristics that are associated with positive adjustment, we divided the widows into categories with respect to personal characteristics, ties to church and neighborhood organizations, and contacts with friends and relatives. Inasmuch as half of the widows had made a stable adjustment, we reasoned that any category where "successful" widows were overrepresented—say, where 60 percent or more manifested stable adjustment—must refer to a characteristic that somehow facilitates adjustment to bereavement. The categories in which 60 percent or more of the widows had achieved stable adjustment are as follows:

Attends church more often now than did before the fire	83%
Participates in church social events	81
Self-perception as "very religious"	77
High education (high school graduate or above)	73
High family income ($11,000 and over in 1972)	71
Group of friends has changed since the fire	67
High participation in community organizations (attended 3 + meetings during past month)	67
Moderate telephone contact with friends (1-2 times in past week)	67
Church members	63
Says that religion has gained in importance in her life since the fire	61
Young age (under 35)	60

Judging from the percentages in the list, it seems that involvement in church activities and perceptions of self as religious person, education, income, and activity in community organizations or in a new friendship group are key predictors of successful adjustment to widowhood. It may also be that some of these factors overlap with others in producing adjustment. For example, it might be that widows active in community organizations are also the better educated and that it is the education rather than the participation in organized groups that produces a stable adjustment.

We again conducted a multiple-regression analysis, assessing the impact of thirteen independent variables on the net adjustment score. Only five of the thirteen made a statistically significant contribution to the variance in net adjustment. They were, in order of degree of influence, education, family income, number of organizational meetings attended in the past month, how religious the respondent perceived herself, and whether her group of friends had changed. Of these five, the first two were the strongest predictors of net change in quality of life. Education by itself accounted for almost half of the variation in life quality explained by all five. Additional details about the multiple-regression analysis have been published elsewhere (Bahr and Harvey 1979) and will not be repeated here.

Summary

The foregoing analysis leads to at least four general conclusions. First, certain demographic characteristics have been highlighted as powerful correlates of the widow's morale or adjustment to widowhood. Education in particular and to a lesser extent income and age have been shown to be key predictors of morale. If the widow has these personal resources to act as buffers against low morale, her social involvement has only slight effect on her outlook. The trio of personal resources of good education, young age, and economic security is found with the widow who has high morale. Conversely, the older, less educated, and poorer widow is likely to have low morale. Frequent contacts with relatives or belonging to many organizations do not seem to be able to compensate for the absence of these personal characteristics.

Second, although a few key variables are highly significant in predicting a widow's morale, these same variables are far less important in predicting morale among the comparison samples. In other words, the condition of widowhood makes some characteristics particularly salient. Education is a prime example. It was not strongly related to perceived happiness or life quality among women in the comparison samples, but it was the single most important predictor of the widow's morale. Moreover, the extent of morale accounted for by the variables we have considered is much higher among widows than among the other women. Apparently, the factors associated with happiness in the general population are more diverse than for widows. Sudden bereavement seems to have enhanced the significance of "fundamentals." Among widows, youth and high educational attainment affect happiness, probably because they are thrown upon their own resources abruptly. In contrast, no such dramatic effect of youth or education on happiness is found within the two control groups; apparently only to widows are such factors important.

Third, religiosity, whether defined as the feeling that one is a religious person or by participation in church worship services or social events, is positively related to a widow's morale, although it is far less important than the widow's education or income in predicting adjustment or happiness scores.

Finally, our data suggests that by six months after the bereavement many widows had made a successful adjustment to their new status. This is not to say that the problems of widowhood were all behind them but rather that they rated their own happiness or life quality as comparable to earlier times in their lives. Their net loss in life quality was now a manageable one or two points as they rate it. A few widows even rated their present situation as better than that experienced at a standard reference point five years previously.

References

Arling, G.T. 1976. "The Elderly Widow and Her Family, Neighbors, and Friends." *Journal of Marriage and the Family* 38:757-768.

Atchley, Robert C. 1975. "Dimensions of Widowhood in Later Life." *The Gerontologist* 15 (April):176-178.

Bahr, Howard M., and Harvey, Carol D. 1979. "Widowhood and Perceptions of Change in Quality of Life: Evidence from the Sunshine Mine Widows." *Journal of Comparative Family Studies* 10 (Autumn).

_____ . 1980. "Correlates of Morale Among the Newly Widowed." *Journal of Social Psychology*. Forthcoming.

Barrett, Carol J. 1977. "Women in Widowhood." *Signs* 2 (Summer): 856-868.

Borgatta, Edgar F. 1968. "My Student, the Purist: A Lament." *Sociological Quarterly* 9 (Winter):29-34.

Carey, Raymond G. 1977. "The Widowed: A Year Later." *Journal of Counseling Psychology* 24 (No. 2):125-131.

Glick, Ira O., Weiss, Robert S. and Parkes, C. Murray. 1974. *The First Year of Bereavement*. New York: Wiley.

Harvey, Carol D., and Bahr, Howard M. 1974. "Widowhood, Morale, and Affiliation." *Journal of Marriage and the Family* 36 (February):97-106.

Labovitz, Sanford. 1967. "Some Observations on Measurement and Statistics." *Social Forces* 46 (December):151-160.

_____ . "The Assignment of Numbers to Ranks." *American Sociological Review* 35 (June):515-525.

_____ . "In Defense of Assigning Numbers to Ranks." *American Sociological Review* 36 (June):521-522.

Lopata, Helena Z. 1970. "The Social Involvement of American Widows." *American Behavioral Scientist* 14 (September-October):41-57.

_____ . *Widowhood in an American City*. Cambridge, Mass.: Schenkman.

Walker, K.N., MacBride, A., and Vachon, M.L.S. 1977. *Social Science and Medicine* 11:35-41.

7 Loneliness

Almost everyone is lonely some of the time. Liability to loneliness seems characteristic of the human condition, and it may be a critically important characteristic. In one view, loneliness is necessary for the creation of society and culture. Loneliness is uncomfortable, and "it coerces us into consorting and communicating." It is thus "a spur that prods us into life" (Hoskisson 1963:11). Loneliness has been designated as a "psychological drive," perhaps even "a universal principle through which we may 'understand' why man does what he does . . ." (Mijuskovic 1977:113-114). It drives us to seek companionship. While that companionship may not satisfy all the needs of which the loneliness is symptom, it creates bonds of interdependence and increases our chances for accomplishment and survival. The insistent drive toward affiliation that loneliness produces, and its capacity to serve as a context for self-discovery and personal development have been portrayed with warmth and empathy by Moustakas (1972, 1975). He affirms its motivating quality in phrases such as "the loneliness each man feels is his hunger for life" and in emphasizing the link between loneliness and self-discovery.

Loneliness is frequently considered a disorder (Fromm-Reichman 1959; Weinburg 1967; Strugnell 1974; Weiss 1973), and it contributes to a variety of other disorders including insomnia, hyperactivity, and various psychosomatic illnesses. Most people find it unpleasant, and for many, loneliness leads not to creation and reaffiliation but to continued alienation and perhaps even death. Ordinary loneliness usually does not lead to self-revelation or greater awareness of one's universal ties to others. It is uncomfortable and apparently unprofitable, and it has received much less scholarly attention than the other varieties. It is

> gnawing rather than ennobling, a chronic distress without redeeming features. . . . Ordinary loneliness is uniformly distressing. . . . In loneliness there is a drive to rid oneself of one's distress by integrating a new relationship or regaining a lost one. . . . The lonely are driven to find others, and if they find the right others, they change and are no longer lonely (Weiss 1973:15).

Reprinted with permission of the publisher from: Howard M. Bahr and Carol D. Harvey, "Correlates of Loneliness among Widows Bereaved in a Mining Disaster," *Psychological Reports*, 44 (1979):367-385.

Hoskisson (1963) has listed various types of loneliness, including general loneliness, which is an unspecified desire for society and companionship; interest loneliness, which is a desire for compatible companionship; nostalgic loneliness, a loneliness for a particular environment or situation or familiar context; faithless loneliness, which is a yearning for a cause, a goal, or a faith; specific loneliness, which is loneliness for a particular individual or a small group; fantasy-specified loneliness, a craving for the ideal or the imagined; incompletion loneliness, the sense of not being fulfilled; the "lost-soul" condition, which is a sense of being cut off and having no spiritual hope; and the "God lonely" state, which involves the sense of being estranged from God. Note that at least four of these types of loneliness may characterize widows who have not only lost husbands but also the social circle to which coupleness was an essential condition for admission. The widow is apt to be particularly susceptible to general loneliness, interest loneliness, the "not being at homeness" of nostalgic loneliness, and the specific loneliness concretely directed to the missing husband.

Research on Loneliness

Norman Bradburn's (1969) *The Structure of Psychological Well-being* includes reports on loneliness from samples of residents of Chicago, Detroit, a suburb of Washington, D.C., and from respondents in two national samples. His findings reveal a marked consistency in the incidence of loneliness among the adult population of these areas, ranging from 23 percent to 27 percent. The interviewing in the Bradburn studies was done in the period 1966-1968. Respondents in each of the samples were asked, "During the past few weeks did you ever feel very lonely or remote from other people?"

A later study by Weiss in which respondents were asked by telephone rather than interviewed and in which the question was reworded to include "During the past week" rather than "During the past few weeks" found 11 percent of the national population reporting loneliness. In contrast to Bradburn's work, Weiss found women to be somewhat more lonely than men. He also found the poor and the ill to be particularly prone to loneliness, and that women over 55 were more likely than others to report loneliness. Among the widowed women in the survey, 29 percent reported loneliness in the past week. The relationship between loneliness and age was found to be curvilinear; that is, there is more loneliness among the very young than the middle-aged, and there is even more among the elderly than among the young (Weiss 1973:26,29).

Glick, Weiss, and Parkes (1974:212, 242-243), in a series of interviews during the thirteen months following bereavement among a sample of widows in Boston, found that loneliness did not fade with time unless reaf-filiation occurred. Three weeks after bereavement, 78 percent of the sample agreed with the statement "I am so lonely." A month later 70 percent agreed, and a year later, 65 percent agreed with the statement. Two to four years later, among women who had remarried or were engaged to be remar-ried, expression of loneliness had declined to near normal levels. Establish-ment of new emotional ties and marriage or plans of marriage were thus related to sharply reduced feelings of loneliness. In contrast, women who had not moved toward remarriage but rather had adopted the widow role as a fairly permanent form of life organization were more apt to admit that they were often lonely.

Lopata's (1973) study of widows in Chicago corroborates Glick's find-ding that loneliness continues long after bereavement. Lopata's widows had been bereaved an average of 11 years, and yet half of them identified loneliness as their most important problem, and another third said it was the second most serious problem they faced. Loneliness meant different things to different classes of widows, and Lopata noted eight specific forms of loneliness in terms of what the women said they were lonely for. These included loneliness for the person of husband, a partner in activities, some-meone around, someone to talk to, someone to care for, someone to do things for, and also a sense that "other people shun me," and feelings of "general loneliness."

Lopata also found that widows who emphasized the role of wife strong-ly, who had been more deeply involved with their husbands than some of the others, were the most likely to emphasize their loneliness. On the other hand, women who ranked the role of mother higher than that of wife were less likely to define loneliness as the major problem of widowhood.

Weiss affirms that loneliness represents a deficit condition of two main types, a deficit state of "emotional isolation" and another of "social isola-tion." Each of these deficits may produce loneliness, and because they are deficit states, it is likely that the loneliness will continue over an extended period unless the deficit state is resolved. That is why loneliness, which is a component of the grief syndrome, continues long after other aspects of grief have ended: "It is a reaction to the absence of the cherished figure rather than to the experience of its loss" (Weiss 1973:16).

Loneliness is such a significant problem of widowhood that in her com-prehensive bibliography on adjustment to widowhood, Strugnell (1974) devotes an entire chapter to the topic. One of the points made in the chapter is that loneliness is related to depression, a finding also recorded by Brad-burn who reported a high correlation between loneliness and depression for both men and women. Strugnell notes also that since depression is related to loss of self-esteem, loneliness and low self-esteem are therefore logically related. Lopata (1969) also links loneliness and self-esteem, although she refers to "inadequacy" rather than low self-esteem. The literature reviewed by Strugnell suggests that loneliness is related to alienation or feelings of being psychologically estranged from others. The tie between loneliness or social isolation and pathology is also reported by Weinberg (1967), especially among individuals whose isolation is either "defensive withdrawal" or "dynamic inability for social relations."

To deal with loneliness/isolation in the short run, Weiss (1973:235) suggests that people learn to tolerate it. In the long run, he recommends locating a network of compatible others and staying in touch with some of its members, directing energy to projects, friendships, or groups one cares about, and developing valid relationships within these groups. His recommendations are similar to Lopata's (1969), who reported that the women she interviewed used three basic techniques to deal with loneliness: keeping busy, developing new roles and relations, and enlarging their own involvement in a single significant role.

This brief review of the research literature on loneliness yields several testable generalizations. They are: (1) Feelings of loneliness during a current or recent period are reported by between one tenth and one fourth of the adult population. (2) Widowed people report loneliness more frequently than the general population. (3) Compared to the general population, loneliness is reported more often by the poor. (4) With respect to age, the old are more frequently lonely than the young, and the young more frequently than the middle-aged. As a logical extension of the advice that people cope with their loneliness by keeping busy, expanding their role set or becoming more intensively involved in selected roles, it follows that loneliness varies inversely with (5) degree of organizational affiliation and participation, with (6) degree of interaction with relatives and friends and with (7) church membership and activity. As for attitudes, (8) loneliness is positively associated with low morale, low self-esteem, and depression. Finally, (9) the more deeply involved a couple as friends and companions, the greater the loneliness of the surviving spouse.

If these generalizations are grouped systematically by variables, there are five categories of possible correlates of loneliness: namely, personal demographic characteristics (2 through 4 above), extent of social network (5 and 6), religious involvement (7), attitudes about self (8), and quality of marriage (9).

Measuring Loneliness

Loneliness among the Sunshine widows was measured directly in an item previously used by Bradburn (1969). It read, "During the past week, how often did you feel very lonely or remote from other people?" The forced-choice responses to this item included "not at all," "once," and "more than once.'' A second measure of loneliness was a yes-no question about the woman's definition of her involvement in the community. It read, ''Are you as involved in community life as you would like to be?'' On the face of it, this second item taps feelings of being left out of the community life, while the first refers more directly to psychological attitudes of being set apart from other people. Some women who think themselves lonely might be satisfied with their community involvement, and some who are unsatisfied with their community network might still not feel lonely. It did seem to us that the desire to be more involved in community life represented one type of loneliness, conceptually different from the psychological feeling of loneliness. In the analysis of correlates of loneliness that follows, we will use both of these indicators of loneliness.

Loneliness and Demographic Characteristics

The distributions of responses to the two indicators of loneliness are given in table 7-1. Note that the extent of loneliness reported by the survivor's wives and other miners' wives is in line with findings in earlier studies,

Table 7-1
Percentage Distribution of Kellogg Women by Loneliness and the Desire for More Community Involvement

Are You as Involved in Community Life as You Would Like to Be?	During the Past Week, How Often did You Feel Very Lonely or Remote from Other People?			
	Not at All	Once	More than Once	Total
Widows (N = 44)				
Yes	9%	14%	43%	66%
No	—	—	34	34
Total	9	14	77	100
Survivors' Wives (N = 48)				
Yes	40	4	17	61
No	23	4	12	39
Total	63	8	29	100
Other Miners' Wives (N = 128)				
Yes	38	11	18	67
No	22	5	6	33
Total	60	16	24	100

although perhaps on the high end of the normal range. The proportions of women in these groups reporting loneliness "more than once" in the past week were 29 and 24 percent, respectively, compared to between one tenth and one fourth of respondents in other surveys. If those who answered "once" were included, we would conclude that rates of reported loneliness in Kellogg were somewhat higher than in other locales where loneliness in the general population has been studied, but it may be that the three-category fixed responses available to our respondents elicited a few "moderate" (that is, "once") replies, which in earlier work using a two-category yes-no format would have been reported as no. In other words, the Kellogg women may manifest loneliness rates at the "high" end of the normal range because of the wider range of possible answers to our item. It may also be that life in a small, somewhat geographically isolated community such as Kellogg fosters feelings of loneliness among some women.

The widows report very high levels of loneliness in comparison to either the other Kellogg groups or to populations studied in previous research on loneliness. More than three-fourths of them reported being lonely "more than once" in the week preceding the interview, a rate approximately three times that of the women in the comparison samples. The notion that expressions of loneliness would be more frequent among widows than in the general population is clearly supported.

Although the widows are much more apt to consider themselves "very lonely or remote from other people" than are other women, note from the percentages in table 7-1 that they are not more apt to feel uninvolved in community life. Their loss has been a deeply personal one, and while it affects their place in the community and the way the members of the community define and treat them, it seems to have little impact on the widows' desire for community involvement. About one third of them said they would like more community involvement, and so did about one third of the women in the comparison samples. With respect to the kind of loneliness represented by feelings of underinvolvement in one's community then, the widows do not differ from other women. Whether widows turn out to be more lonely than other people depends on the type of loneliness being considered.

Now consider the effects of income on feelings of loneliness and underinvolvement. Table 7-2 presents percentages of women reporting loneliness or underinvolvement in the community for variously defined subsamples. The relationship between poverty and loneliness, for example, may be evaluated by reference to the section on "personal characteristics" in each of these tables. Women in families with less than $7,000 annual income in 1972 were not noticeably more lonely or more underinvolved than were women in higher income families. Poverty may make one lonely, but it cannot be shown to do so among our respondents. Perhaps it only makes a difference at very low family incomes, and there were not enough of those in the three Kellogg samples to permit a more refined test of the hypothesis. We can accordingly conclude only that respondents with relatively low incomes do not appear particularly lonely.

Also relevant to the expected linkage between loneliness and poverty is the bearing of perceived or relative income on feelings of loneliness. In contrast to the situation with absolute income, here we find direct positive finding. Loneliness is related to dissatisfaction with family income; in each of the three samples, the most dissatisfied are also the most apt to say they are lonely. The pattern is most striking in the two comparison samples in which loneliness is not so frequent as among the widows.

The consistent pattern that characterized loneliness and satisfaction with family income does not appear for community involvement. While objective low income is not associated with feelings of either loneliness or community underinvolvement, feelings of dissatisfaction with income are strongly related to feelings of personal loneliness but not to feelings of underinvolvement in community affairs.

Now consider another personal demographic characteristic listed in table 7-2, age. It was anticipated that the old would be more lonely than the young, and the young more lonely than the middle-aged. The sample size for widows and survivors' wives is too small to permit a meaningful division into the young, the middle-aged, and the old, and so we used a two-category age division at age 36, essentially splitting the sample into young adults and middle-aged adults. In line with previous research women aged 35 and over were expected to be somewhat less lonely than the younger respondents. This expectation was not supported. Neither loneliness nor community involvement is related to age among these women. In five of the six comparisons (three for loneliness and three for community involvement), the women under 35 have a slightly higher rate of loneliness, but typically the differences are small and do not reach statistical significance.

Several demographic characteristics (education, having been married before, duration of marriage, and employment status) are included in table 7-2 on an exploratory basis. We did not have specific previous research on which to base a hypothesis, but because these variables had been linked to women's happiness or widows' adjustment in previous chapters, we contrasted the rates of reported loneliness and underinvolvement among subsamples divided on the basis of these variables. For the widows, education has a dramatic relationship to loneliness. Almost every widow with less than a high school education said she was lonely, compared to less than half of those who were high school graduates or had higher educational attainment. The same kind of differential appeared for community involvement with 45 percent of widows with less than high school education desiring more community involvement, compared to only 13 percent of the widows who had graduated from high school. This relationship between education

Table 7-2
Percent of Women Having Various Characteristics Reporting Themselves Lonely or Underinvolved in Community Life

Characteristics	Widows			Survivors' Wives			Other Miners' Wives		
	Percent Lonely	Percent Under-involved	Percentage Base (N)	Percent Lonely	Percent Under-involved	Percentage Base (N)	Percent Lonely	Percent Under-involved	Percentage Base (N)
Personal Characteristics									
Age									
Under 35	80	35	(20)	36	45	(22)	23	40	(62)
35 and over	75	33	(24)	22	37	(27)	26	26	(66)
Education									
Less than high school graduate	93	45	(29)	33	44	(24)	22	34	(67)
High school graduate or more	47[a]	13[a]	(15)	24	38	(25)	26	31	(61)
Years married									
0-10	80	35	(20)	29	40	(21)	28	43	(47)
11-45	75	33	(24)	29	41	(28)	22	27	(81)
Married before									
Yes	77	41	(22)	29	36	(14)	32	32	(38)
No	77	27	(22)	29	43	(35)	22	32	(88)
Presently employed									
Yes	80	27	(15)	18	35	(17)	31	27	(26)
No	76	38	(29)	34	44	(32)	23	34	(100)
Family income (1972)									
Less than $7,000	73	33	(15)	29	40	(14)	33	33	(18)
$7,000 +	78	30	(27)	29	41	(35)	23	32	(107)
Social Involvement									
Hours spent in "other leisure activities" yesterday									
0	80	25	(20)	19	38	(16)	28	38	(50)
1-12	74	39	(23)	33	42	(33)	22	29	(78)
Number of organization meetings attended in the past month									
0	81	38	(21)	24	52	(29)	30	35	(74)
1+	76	33	(21)	39	28	(18)	16	23	(43)

Number of organizational affiliations									
0	86	41	(22)	27	54	(26)	32	38	(53)
1	78	33	(9)	18	27	(11)	17	37	(41)
2+	58	25	(12)	42	25	(12)	18	21	(33)
Summary social contact score (relatives and friends)									
0-4	69	19	(16)	29	43	(21)	28	31	(39)
5-8	87	33[a]	(15)	13	50	(15)	22	42	(45)
9-18	77	54	(13)	45	33	(11)	23	23	(43)
Friends changed since disaster									
Yes	67	38	(21)	43	43	(14)	16	63	(19)
No	87	30	(23)	23	40	(35)	26	28[a]	(108)
Socially active before the fire									
Yes	78	31	(32)	30	33	(33)	22	32	(96)
No	70	40	(10)	25	56	(16)	31	34	(32)
Had close friends before the fire									
Yes	78	32	(37)	30	40	(43)	25	30	(111)
No	67	50	(6)	17	50	(6)	18	53	(17)
Hours watched television yesterday									
0-1	73	36	(22)	38	48	(21)	17	30	(47)
2-9	82	32	(22)	22	37	(27)	28	35	(81)
Religious Activity									
Belongs to a church									
Yes	67	30	(27)	40	45	(20)	23	29	(79)
No	94[a]	41	(17)	21	38	(29)	26	39	(49)
Religiosity (salience)									
Very religious	69	31	(13)	33	22	(9)	27	27	(30)
Somewhat, not very, or not at all religious	80	33	(30)	28	45	(40)	23	35	(98)
Church attendance									
Every week, nearly every week, or at least monthly	68	29	(28)	50	45	(22)	21	28	(67)
Less often	94[a]	44	(16)	11	37	(27)	28	38	(61)

Table 7-2 *(continued)*

Characteristics	Widows			Survivors' Wives			Other Miners' Wives		
	Percent Lonely	Percent Under-involved	Percentage Base (N)	Percent Lonely	Percent Under-involved	Percentage Base (N)	Percent Lonely	Percent Under-involved	Percentage Base (N)
Participates in church social events									
Yes	62	25	(16)	70	50	(10)	29	26	(38)
No	86	39	(28)	22[a]	34	(32)	20	34	(85)
Importance of religion since the disaster									
Gained	70	30	(23)	29	35	(21)	28	37	(43)
Lost or stayed the same	86	38	(21)	30	43	(27)	23	29	(82)
Attitudes									
Satisfaction with family income									
Very satisfied	75	33	(12)	13	27	(15)	12	44	(32)
Somewhat satisfied	70	30	(20)	32	44	(25)	25[a]	30	(76)
Dissatisfied	92	42	(12)	44	56	(9)	40	25	(20)
Satisfaction with community									
Very satisfied	86	29	(21)	33	36	(24)	20	30	(60)
Somewhat satisfied	80	50	(10)	22	35	(18)	25	34	(44)
Dissatisfied	58	33	(12)	29	71	(7)	35	39	(23)
Satisfaction with daily work									
Very satisfied	83	8	(12)	12	24	(17)	17	32	(53)
Somewhat satisfied	67	44	(18)	38	62	(21)	31	22	(32)
Dissatisfied	86	43	(14)	36	27	(11)	29	43	(42)
Amount of time spent worrying									
A lot	96	41	(22)	35	37	(20)	48	39	(44)
Not very much, or never worries	59[a]	27	(22)	24	43	(29)	12[a]	29	(82)
Present happiness									
Very happy, pretty happy[b]	53	16	(19)	15	33	(20)	4	36	(44)
Not too happy	96[a]	42	(24)	38	46	(29)	35[a]	31	(84)

Present quality of life score[c]								
1-5	100	45	(22)	43	50	(14)	38	46	(26)
6-7	62[a]	25	(16)	25	56	(16)	17	34	(47)
8-10	33	17	(6)	21	21[a]	(19)	24	25	(55)

Quality of Marriage

Degree of "close personal friendship" with husband								
Very close	81	33	(36)	21	44	(38)	19	32	(93)
Somewhat close, could be better	62	38	(8)	55[a]	30	(11)	38	35	(34)

Note: Women reporting themselves lonely answered "more than once" when asked, "During the past week, how often did you feel lonely or remote from other people?" Women reporting themselves underinvolved in community life answered no or "don't know" when asked, "Are you as involved in community life as you would like to be?" There were no "don't know" responses among the widows or survivors' wives, and only three among the other miners' wives.

[a]Percentage differences are significant at the .05 level.

[b]For survivors' wives and other miners' wives, this category included only the "very happy"; women who answered "pretty happy" were included in the "low" category with the "not too happy."

[c]The item on present quality of life was: "Here is a picture of a ladder. Suppose we say that the top of the ladder (10) represents the best possible life for you and the bottom (1) represents the worst possible life for you. Where on the ladder do you feel you personally stand at the present time?"

and loneliness did not appear in the comparison samples, among whom the difference between the nongraduates and the high school graduates was never more than 9 percentage points and was usually much less than that. The association between education upon widow's loneliness is an illustration of the apparent buffering influence of education on adjustment to widowhood. The better-educated widows seem to cope with their problems more effectively, have more positive self-concepts, feel more tied into the community, and are more apt to feel that others take an interest in them.

We anticipated that length of marriage would be related to feelings of loneliness among the widows because a long-term relationship would presumably be a deeper one with more years of shared experience to draw on and hence more sense of irreplaceable loss when it ended abruptly. For the other samples we had no reason to expect a pattern in either direction. The findings, shown in table 7-2, are that length of marriage has no effect on feelings of loneliness among women in any of the samples. With one exception (feelings of underinvolvement among other miners' wives), the differences between women married ten years or less and those married for 11 years or longer are of the order of 6 percent or less, and so it was concluded that length of marriage was not an important predictor of loneliness.

In all three samples, employed women are slightly less likely than other women to express feelings of underinvolvement in the community. However, employment status seems to have no consistent effect on feelings of loneliness; the small differences in reports of loneliness between working and nonworking women appear to be random fluctuations. Similarly, there does not seem to be any consistent pattern in the slight variations in loneliness and feelings of underinvolvement in community life between women who had been married before and those whose present (or last, in the case of the widows) marriage was their first.

In conclusion, an analysis of the apparent effects of selected personal characteristics on rates of reported loneliness and underinvolvement suggests that only two variables, satisfaction with family income and educational attainment, have much bearing on the two kinds of loneliness. The effects of education are limited to the widows and apply to both community underinvolvement and loneliness. The effects of satisfaction with family income appear to affect women generally but only with respect to personal loneliness and not to community underinvolvement.

Loneliness and Social Involvement

The general principle underlying our expectations about the effects of organization participation and contact with relatives and friends is that social involvement is an antidote to loneliness. It is presumed that the active do not have time to be lonely. The second panel of table 7-2 contains nine indicators of social involvement, including two in which direct involvement with other persons is ambiguous, namely, the items on hours of the day preceding the interview spent watching television or spent in "other leisure activities" (that is, other than television watching and reading). Operating on the assumption that television watching is less "social" than the possible "other leisure activities," we tentatively predicted a positive relationship between hours spent watching television and loneliness and an inverse relationship between hours of other leisure and loneliness. For the other seven indicators the direction of the expected relationship was inverse: the more the activity, the less the loneliness.

The findings, unfortunately, are ambiguous. For only one of the nine indicators of social involvement is the direction of a relationship consistent across the three samples. For that one—the affirmation that before the fire the respondent had close friends in the community—the differences in rates of reported loneliness are too small to be taken seriously. Aspects of social involvement that seem unrelated to widows' loneliness include number of organizational meetings attended in the past month, social contact with friends and relatives, extent of social activity and friendship with other women in the community before the fire, and extent of present television viewing. The social involvement variables that are associated with variations in widows' loneliness are memberships in voluntary organizations and whether one's group of friends has changed since the fire. (Note in table 7-2 the clear and statistically significant reduction in the proportion of lonely women as the number of organizational affiliations increases, and note also that women with new friends are less lonely than those whose friends stayed the same.) The survivors' wives manifest some unusual patterns with respect to loneliness; those who belong to organizations and attend many meetings are lonelier than those who do not; and those whose group of friends has changed are, unlike the widows, *more* lonely.

There is a consistent pattern in the relationship between social activity and feelings of being underinvolved in the community. In every sample the women with one or more memberships and with some meeting attendance are less apt to feel left out of community life than those with no memberships or meeting attendance.

Variables having no consistent association with feelings of underinvolvement in the community are hours spent in other leisure activities, whether the woman was socially active before the fire, hours spent watching television, and whether the relationship with her husband was (is) perceived as close. For the widows but not the other women there is a strong inverse relation between contact with friends and relatives and feelings of underinvolvement in the community; those who had the most such contact were those who felt underinvolved.

Two variables for which there were modest and consistent differences were the item on whether the women's group of friends had changed since the fire and the item on whether the woman had close friendship ties with women in the community before the fire. Women who said their friends had changed were more apt to feel underinvolved than the others, especially among other miners' wives; women with no close friendship ties before the fire were the most apt to feel underinvolved in the community.

Whether loneliness and activity are related, it turns out, depends on the type of loneliness and the type of activity under consideration.

Church Membership and Activity

The predicted inverse relationship between church activity and loneliness is supported by our findings for the widows only. In other words, the inverse relationship between church activity and loneliness holds for a particularly troubled (bereaved) population, but apparently it does not hold for the general population. The third panel of table 7-2 contains five measures of religious activity or salience. In every case, five times out of five, the "high religiosity" category of widows manifests less loneliness than the other category. The difference is greatest for church membership and attendance; in each case two thirds of the members or fairly regular attenders say they are lonely, compared to almost all (94 percent) of those who do not belong or who attend infrequently. Admittedly, most of the differences are not large enough to reach statistical significance, but the pattern is entirely consistent.

For the other miners' wives religion has little bearing on loneliness, and for the survivors' wives the direction of the relationship is opposite from that anticipated: Survivors' wives who belong to a church, attend church often, and participate in church social events, are *more* apt to report loneliness than survivors' wives who do not. Despite this perplexing finding for the survivors' wives, it is plain that widows who attend church and perceive themselves as religious are less lonely than other widows.

The same pattern appears when the dependent variable is feelings of underinvolvement in community life. For each of the five measures of religious activity, the widows who are "high" on religiosity or religious participation are less apt to feel left out of community life than the others. There is no clear pattern among the survivors' wives. Among the other miners' wives, the direction of the relationship is as anticipated, but the effects of religious activity seem to be fairly weak. None of the differences between the high and low religiosity subsamples are greater than 10 percent.

In summary, the hypothesized inverse relationship between church activity and loneliness does appear for the widows. It applies to both measures of loneliness, community underinvolvement and a personal perception of being lonely. The absence of a consistent significant relationship between loneliness and church activity in the other samples suggests that the relationship exists for the widows because of the role of the church and religion in helping them to deal with bereavement.

Loneliness, Morale, and Quality of Marriage

According to our review of previous research the negative attitude of loneliness is associated with other dimensions of unhappiness. Inspection of the appropriate panel of table 7-2 reveals that there is no consistent relationship between loneliness and satisfaction with community, daily work, or family income. There is a strong and consistent relationship between loneliness and more direct indicators of personal happiness, namely, perceived quality of life, present happiness, and amount of time spent worrying. That loneliness is a major factor underlying the women's, especially the widows', perceptions of personal happiness and well-being is apparent in the nine comparisons, one for each sample for the items on worry, present happiness, and quality of life, shown in table 7-2. In every case the percentage lonely is highest among those who worry, consider themselves "not too happy," or consider their present quality of life to be low. *All* of the widows who rated their quality of life in the low category (scores 1-5 on the 10-point scale) said they were lonely "more than once" during the week before the interview; and 96 percent of those who said they worried "a lot" were lonely.

The same pattern is apparent when the measure of loneliness is feelings of underinvolvement in the community, although the findings are neither as strong nor as consistent. Among the survivors' wives and other miners' wives, there is a very modest tendency for those dissatisfied with the community to express a desire for more involvement in it, and among the widows those who are satisfied with their daily work are least apt to feel underinvolved in the community. The unhappy, the most worried, and those having the lowest life-quality scores are the most apt to feel underinvolved. Since there are fewer statistical differences in feelings of underinvolvement in community between women who are happy and unhappy and between those who see their lives as high instead of low in quality, the data suggest that feelings of community involvement have much less to do with morale than do feelings of personal loneliness.

Both the survivors' wives and the other miners' wives are different from the widows in that it is the women who do not have a close friendship relationship with their husbands who are lonely, while among the widows the lonely are the ones who had such a relationship and lost it. Hypothesis 9 is therefore supported for the direct measure of loneliness. Feelings of underinvolvement in the community show no relationship to perceived quality of personal relationship to husband, however. It is plain that in specifying correlates of loneliness, it makes a big difference what kind of loneliness is being measured. Generalized loneliness is not the same as loneliness for specific kinds of ties or particular persons.

Summary

The rates of loneliness reported by women in the comparison samples are roughly congruent with those reported in other surveys on the topic, and, as anticipated, the widows manifested extremely high levels of personal loneliness. Widows did not reveal extraordinary rates of perceived community isolation or underinvolvement. We are thus alerted to the possibility that the loneliness of the widows was fairly specific and did not extend to perceptions of being left out of the community life.

The hypothesized links between low income and loneliness or community underinvolvement did not appear. It may be that such a relationship pertains to the very poor, but the present research was not designed to interview sufficient numbers of people in poverty to produce reliable findings. Dissatisfaction with income was moderately related to personal loneliness but not to feelings of community involvement. There was also no evidence of associations between age and loneliness or feelings of underinvolvement in the community.

Some aspects of organizational affiliation and participation were related to loneliness. The most striking relationship was for the number of affiliations; widows with many memberships were much less lonely than those with few, and widows with few affiliations were less lonely than those with none. The same pattern appeared for feelings of involvement in the community, with widows who said they felt underinvolved being much less apt to belong to many organizations. There was also a consistent, direct relationship between contact with relatives and friends and feelings of belonging in the community, but not feelings of personal loneliness. In addition, widows whose friendship group had changed, that is, those who had acquired new friends, were less likely than others to report themselves lonely, but there was no consistent patterns with respect to new friends and feelings of community involvement.

The finding of an inverse relationship between religious participation and loneliness was substantial and consistent. Among the widows, for every indicator of religious salience or participation, the more religious were less lonely than the others. This pattern did not appear among the comparison samples, and it applies primarily to personal feelings of loneliness; religious participation was not nearly as strongly linked to widows' feelings of community involvement.

The anticipated positive association between loneliness and dissatisfaction with specific aspects of life such as work and community dissatisfaction did not appear. There was a dramatic association between loneliness and several indicators of morale, namely, happiness, amount of time spent worrying, and perceived quality of life. The direct tie between loneliness and low morale was also apparent in the comparison samples. Feelings of community underinvolvement were much less consistently related to the indicators of morale, but among the widows the percentage distributions were in the expected direction even though not statistically significant.

Finally the hypothesis that the quality of marriage is associated with perceptions of loneliness following bereavement was supported. Widows who reported a high quality, "close" relationship with their husbands were more lonely than the others. The quality of the former marital relationship had no bearing on feelings of community underinvolvement, however.

The foregoing review of findings suggests three main conclusions. First, it appears that there are many dimensions of loneliness, and researchers and clinicians need to distinguish among its specific types and components. Even the indicator of personal loneliness used in the present study, with its reference to the state of being "very lonely or remote from other people," needs to be broken into several questions with specific referent individuals or classes of persons. Certainly the feelings of being cut off or remote should be distinguished from a personal longing for specific individuals or classes of persons, and yet the item as it stands includes both.

A second conclusion is that the two dimensions we have measured do reveal a distinctive set of correlates. Feelings of not belonging or underinvolvement in a community are conceptually a type of loneliness, but the antecedents and correlates of these feelings of isolation from community life are clearly different from those for the kind of loneliness, measured by the question of whether the respondent felt "very lonely or remote from other people." It follows that those who treat or study the lonely should recognize that the appropriate prescriptions for loneliness of the "community isolation" type may differ from those that apply to the personally lonely type.

Finally, judging from our correlational analysis, it appears that some of the commonly advised "cures" for loneliness may not be effective for certain types of loneliness. For example, with respect to personal loneliness, increased contacts with friends and relatives or increased exposure to television or involvement in various "other leisure" pursuits may not help much. More likely to be effective is increased participation in a variety of formal organizations, particularly increased involvement in churches and religious organizations. The very best prescription for loneliness of this type may be a preventive one: It will be remembered that the widows who were relatively well educated were much less apt than the others to say that they were lonely.

The well-educated widows were also less likely to report feelings of community isolation. In addition, frequent contact with friends and relatives, belonging to a variety of organizations, having satisfying daily employment, and participating in religious organizations were associated with low levels of community isolation. Both types of loneliness are correlated with general morale, happiness, and perceived high quality of life among widows, but the relationships are much more dramatic for the personal loneliness than for community underinvolvement. In the comparison samples personal loneliness but not community underinvolvement is also highly correlated to general morale.

The high correlations between perceived loneliness and morale, and presumably to mental health generally, suggest a need for much more research on the varieties and the specific correlates of loneliness. The two types of loneliness considered in the present chapter are only a beginning. A variety of types of loneliness should be charted empirically, and the relationships among them as well as the correlates of each ought to be documented. Perhaps then will we be able to dispute Weiss's (1973:28) criticism that it is the songwriters rather than the social scientists who have taught us about loneliness.

References

Bradburn, N.M. 1969. *The Structure of Psychological Well-Being.* Chicago: Aldine.

Fromm-Reichmann, F. 1959. "Loneliness." *Psychiatry* 22:1-15.

Glick, I.O., Weiss, R.S., and Parkes, C.M. 1974. *The First Year of Bereavement.* New York: Wiley.

Hoskisson, J.B. 1963. *Loneliness: An Explanation, a Cure.* New York: Citadel Press.

Lopata, H.Z. 1969. "Loneliness: Forms and Components." *Social Problems* 17:248-262.

———. 1973. *Widowhood in an American City.* Cambridge, Mass.: Schenkman.

Mijuskovic, B. 1977. "Loneliness: An interdisciplinary approach." *Psychiatry* 40:113-132.

Moustakas, C.E. 1972. *Loneliness and Love.* Englewood Cliffs, N.J.: Prentice-Hall.

———. 1975. *The Touch of Loneliness.* Englewood Cliffs, N.J.: Prentice-Hall.

Strugnell, C. 1974. *Adjustment to Widowhood and Some Related Problems.* New York: Health Sciences Publishing.

Weinberg, S.K. 1967. "The Relevance of the Forms of Isolation to Schizophrenia." *International Journal of Social Psychiatry* 13:33-41.

Weiss, R.S. 1973. *Loneliness: The Experience of Emotional and Social Isolation.* Cambridge, Mass.: MIT Press, 1973.

8 Widowhood in Retrospect: Five Years Later

In 1977 we conducted a second study of the Sunshine Mine widows. The 1972 survey had focused on adjustment to widowhood during the first six months; the 1977 study was more concerned with the long-term adaptations to bereavement and with perceptions of life as widows. As a result some of the findings may be more applicable to widows generally than was the case with the initial study.

The 1977 five-year follow-up study was supported by a research grant from the state of Idaho. Its methods generally paralleled those of the 1972 survey. An attempt was made to locate all of the women widowed in the Sunshine Mine fire and to interview them in their homes. As before, interviewers were trained local women. Interviewer training was also the same as in the 1972 study.

The modest scale of the research grant did not permit intensive follow-up of widows who had moved far from the Coeur d'Alene River Valley. In all we were able to find addresses for 65 of the 77 women widowed in the fire. Forty-five of these lived in the Coeur d'Alene River Valley, and 27 of these 45 consented to interviews. A questionnaire form of the instrument mailed to the out-of-state women produced one additional written response; two widows lived in other parts of Idaho where the senior author could conduct the interview. Data were thus obtained from 30 of 65 potential respondents. These 30 represent 39 percent of all Sunshine widows and 64 percent of those who remained in Idaho.

The personal characteristics of these 30 widows were as follows: They had lived in the Coeur d'Alene River Valley for a median of 24 years, with a range of 1 to 61 years. Seventy-three percent of them had kin living in the Kellogg area. Their median age was 41, with a range from 25 to 75. Sixty-three percent had completed some high school or were high school graduates. Their number of children ranged from zero to eight. Thirty-seven percent were employed for wages outside the home. Their annual family incomes ranged from $3,000 to $25,000 with the median in the $11,000-$12,000 category. Sixteen of them (53 percent) had remarried.

Perceptions, Advice, Help, and Compensations

Following the lead of Lopata (1973), there was a series of questions that had to do with perceptions of widowhood itself, advice they would give to new widows, help they had received during widowhood, and compensations if any, or being a widow.

Perceptions of Widowhood

To obtain a subjective judgment about widowhood itself, we asked, "Many women have said that they change after becoming a widow. How has this been for you?" Half of the women answered in terms of increased personal independence, as follows:

> I had to make decisions, learn to drive, be aggressive, ignore criticism, and raise the kids my way.

> There was a big change. You have to handle everything. I had never worked before. Household expenses were a big problem to me. I have to learn to handle other people.

> I have changed. I used to be real quiet and let people walk all over me. Not any more.

> Yes, I've changed in the respect of having to look out for myself. I have become more alert to things around me.

These statements illustrate the response of resocialization and may fit into either the continuity or replacement modes of adaptation to widowhood described in chapter 4.

In contrast, seven of the widows (23 percent) said that widowhood had made them *less* independent, saying,

> I'm more dependent. I don't have the security that I had before.

> I am more cautious.

> I was a very dependent person before. I have become more dependent. I picked up a lot of habits from my husband that I thought I never would.

Two widows (7 percent) said there had been no change. One said, "No, it didn't change me. I had five little ones at home and I went on." The other said, "No, I don't think I've changed so much." These two seem to personify the "continuity" adaptation to widowhood.

There were a variety of other responses, most of which would seem to fit the withdrawal/disaffiliation mode of adjustment in chapter 4. Sample responses in this category include these:

> It's hard to be a mother and father both. I'm awfully snappy.

> I developed an ulcer.

> After I was a widow I was in shock so much. I had so many things to take care of. . . . There have been too many pressures for me to cope with.

The same feeling of independence that was noted by half of the subjects on the free-response question on change after widowhood was also reflected in their answers to some fixed-response questions. Seventy-three percent of the 30 widows agreed with the statement, "A widow has to make her own life and not depend upon others." Sixty-six percent agreed that "The hardest thing for a widow to learn is how to make decisions."

There was considerable agreement about other problems of widowhood. Sixty-seven percent of the widows agreed that "One problem of being a widow is feeling like a 'fifth wheel';" 57 percent said that "People take advantage of you when they know you are a widow," and 60 percent agreed that "Other women are jealous of a widow when their husbands are around."

Despite the evidence of a relationship between high morale and having a new circle of friends for widows, which we mentioned in chapter 6, the five-year follow-up reveals widows being loyal to past ties. Seventy percent agreed that "Old friends cannot be replaced no matter how one tries to make new friends." Fifty-six percent agreed that "A new widow should not move too soon from the place in which she was living before her husband died." All of these fixed-response items produced results comparable to those reported by Lopata in 1973 for Chicago widows.

Help in Coping with Widowhood

When asked if some person was particularly helpful in assisting with coping with widowhood, most subjects (77 percent) said yes. Friends and relatives were mentioned the most frequently, and the biggest contributions a confidant made were to keep a widow busy or to be someone with whom to talk. Indicative of the importance of the listener role were the following responses:

> She was always there. I talked and she listened. She helped get me back in school. She had not been through it but seemed to know how to help.

> She was always there when I needed her to listen, a shoulder to cry on. She was divorced and had problems of her own.

> He was always right there when needed. You can talk to him confidentially and know it won't go any further.

Indicative of the help that kept widows busy were these responses:

> . . . by keeping me busy and keeping my mind off him.

We're very close, she and I. She told me I shouldn't sit at home but get out.

She pushed me ahead, helped me quit living in the past, made me be with people. She bodily pushed me.

Advice to a New Widow

We can gain further insight into the problems these widows faced by examining their statements about how they would counsel other widows. The most frequent advice, mentioned by one third of the women, was that widows should keep busy. Here are some specific admonitions:

Get out. Go to school or work as a volunteer. Get around other people. Find someone to talk to.

Go to work. That way she can be with other people, and not sit home and feel sorry for herself.

Although I couldn't take this advice, I'd say, "Don't sit home and mope." The worst thing in the world is just sitting.

Keep busy—get involved in new things.

Other widows strongly recommended action reflecting personal independence. One said, "If they thought something was right, go ahead and do it. Use their own judgment on things." On the other hand, more frequent were suggestions that new widows be cautious and take things slowly:

Stick close with your family. You're not in mental capacity.

Don't remarry for over a year, until you are established and get to know them better.

Sit back and beware of people borrowing money.

Be very, very careful who you are around, talk to, and what you do.

Watch your money. Don't let people take advantage of you.

When asked, "What do you think is the single most important problem of widowhood?", 12 widows mentioned raising children by themselves. These women said they were apt to be "overindulgent, trying to make up for the loss of the children's father," or to be "too willing to give in to childrens' wishes or demands."

The second most commonly mentioned problem, loneliness, was suggested by eight widows. Although Lopata's (1973) subjects mentioned loneliness more often than problems with raising children, we think that the difference between her results and the Sunshine widows' perceptions we have recorded is probably due to age. The Sunshine widows were younger and were more apt to face rearing young children alone as a consequence of their widowhood. Other problems mentioned as "most important" included the difficulty of making one's own decisions on finances, of not having another adult around, and of having feelings of insecurity.

Compensations of Widowhood

Continuing to following the line of questioning suggested by Lopata (1973), we asked "What advantages or compensations does a widow have which a married women does not have?" Half of the subjects mentioned independence of time and decisions as follows:

> They can come and go as they please. You're not into a routine.

> I didn't have to be anywhere or have any certain schedule.

> I enjoy my life. I feel I can buy a $100 outfit without feeling guilty. I can get up any time I want on Saturday morning.

> You aren't contradicted when you do something.

That such "advantages" of widowhood were not appreciated by many of the women was apparent in the response of the one widow in three who could mention *no* compensations. Some illustration of that third are these:

> None that I can think of. I didn't think I was being blessed by being a widow.

> Right now I can't think of anything. You have to be awful careful to let people know you are alone.

> None. It's really scary.

Morale and Happiness

The 1977 survey contained the same questions on quality of life and perceived happiness that were considered at length in chapters 5 and 6. Comparisons of the widow's responses to these items in 1972 and 1977 permit some conclusions about long-range changes in widows' morale. The percentage distributions of responses to the 10-step "ladder of life quality" question at the time of the interview five years before and five years in the future are given in table 8-1. In making the 1972-1977 comparisons, it should be remembered that not all of the 1977 respondents were interviewed in 1972. In each study we tried to interview all available widows of victims of the Sunshine fire. A few of those available in 1977 were not in the 1972 survey, and over one third of those interviewed in 1972 are not among the 30 questioned in 1977. In other words, not all of the 30 respondents in 1977 can be matched directly to women in the 1972 study; nevertheless, it is legitimate to compare rates or distributions for the two groups as a whole to represent the aggregate group of Sunshine widows at two different times.

The results in table 8-1 support several conclusions. First, the widows of 1977 are indeed happier than they were in 1972. Whereas in 1972 half of them had estimated a low present quality of life (scores of 5 or less on the 10-point scale), only one fourth had such low scores in 1977. Second, the widows' perceptions about how bad things were in 1972 are considerably worse in retrospect than they were perceived to be at the time. Asked about quality of life five years ago, 87 percent of the Sunshine widows in 1977 estimated their own life-quality scores at that time on level 5 or less on the 10-step scale, while in 1972 half of them had estimated their present quality of life at 6 or above. We made the point in chapter 5 that in 1972 the widows idealized their past quality of life; in 1977, remembering the year of widowhood, they idealized in a negative direction, recalling things as worse than they had reported them at the time. Finally, the widows were optimistic both in 1972 and 1977 with respect to the future. In 1972 three fourths of them expected that in five years they would be enjoying a very high quality of life (8-10 on the 10-point scale). The 1977 estimates of present life quality permit us to answer the question of whether their optimism was justified. It appears that some of them must have been disappointed, for only 30 percent said they had achieved a life quality in the 8+ range; nevertheless, in 1977 they still manifested the same degree of optimism with 80 percent anticipating a future life quality in that high range.

In addition to looking at the five-year changes, we assessed the effects of selected personal characteristics on present life quality. For the 1977 sample, health, employment status, and education were strong predictors of high life quality. Widows who said their health was excellent or good, who were employed, or who were at least high school graduates were more than twice as likely as other widows to report high scores (7-10) on present quality of life. Seventy-nine percent of the widows who said their present health was "good" or better also claimed a high life quality, compared to 36 percent of those with "fair" or "poor" health; 85 percent of the employed had high life quality, compared to 43 percent of the nonemployed; and 88 per-

Table 8-1
Perceived Quality of Life for Present, Past, and Future of Widows, in 1972 and 1977

Quality of Life	Score of Quality	1972 %		1977 %	
At present	0	—		—	
	1	14		3	
	2	—		—	
	3	—	50	3	26
	4	9		7	
	5	27		13	
	6	18		10	
	7	18		33	
	8	7		10	
	9	5	14	10	30
	10	2		10	
Total[a]		100		99	
(N)		(44)		(30)	
Five years ago	0	—		7	
	1	2		47	
	2	2		3	
	3	5	20	13	87
	4	2		10	
	5	9		7	
	6	11		—	
	7	5		3	
	8	7		3	
	9	20	63	7	10
	10	36		—	
Total[a]		99		100	
(N)		(44)		(30)	
Five years from now	0	—		7	
	1	3		—	
	2	—		—	
	3	—	16	—	17
	4	3		7	
	5	10		3	
	6	3		—	
	7	8		3	
	8	13		20	
	9	21	74	17	80
	10	40		43	
Total[a]		101		100	
(N)		(44)		(30)	

Note: The items on quality of life were the questions, "Where on the ladder do you feel you personally stand at the present time, five years ago, and five years from now?" Scores ranged from 0 (low) to 10 (high).

[a]Percentages do not always total 100 due to rounding.

cent of the widows who had at least completed high school had a high life quality versus 38 percent for those with less formal schooling.

Remember that on the 1972 survey, education and income were associated with estimates of life quality. Income did not turn out to be a significant correlate with life quality in 1977, but it did affect both perceived happiness and loneliness levels as is reported below.

Perceived happiness was measured by asking the widow, "Taken all together, how would you say things are these days? Would you say you are happy, pretty happy, or not too happy?" In 1972 the percentage of widows who responded "not too happy" was 56; by 1977 only 27 percent felt that way. Perceptions of happiness were related to income, age, and health. The widows who were the happiest in 1977 were those with higher incomes, younger age, and better health. Education and age had been important correlates of happiness in 1972; however, in 1977 education was not significantly related to perceived happiness. Apparently, its effects as a buffer variable, helping widows to adjust to widowhood, had run its course by 1977. Remember that within the comparison samples in 1972, education was also unrelated to perceived happiness.

Self-Esteem and Loneliness

Widowhood can bring about dramatic changes in how a woman views herself. A major source of validation of the self, the husband, is lost, and subsequent effects on the survivor's self-image may be quite drastic. Both the 1972 and 1977 surveys contained several self-esteem items in the form of descriptive statements with which the women agreed or disagreed. In 1972 about half of the widows consistently gave low self-esteem answers. By 1977 the incidence of negative self-definitions of the same items had sharply declined. On only one item, "I certainly feel useless at times," was there still a substantial proportion of widows who agreed and thereby gave a negative response. See table 8-2 for a summary of self-esteem items.

In line with their apparent successful adaptation to widowhood over the five-year period, the widows in 1977 reported much less loneliness. Only one in four of them said they had felt lonely "more than once" in the preceding week, compared to three in four in 1972. The 1977 survey had an additional indicator of loneliness: "Some of the people we talk to speak of being lonely. Would you say that you are lonely often, sometimes, seldom, or never?" Twenty-three percent of the widows said "often," 38 percent "sometimes," and 44 percent "seldom or never."

Several personal characteristics were strongly associated with feelings of loneliness among the widows in 1977. Widows who were young, healthy, remarried, or employed or who had high incomes were the ones who typically reported low levels of loneliness. The characteristic that seemed to

Table 8-2

Percentage of Widows Giving the "Low" Self-Esteem Response on Items about Self, in 1972 and 1977

Item	1972	1977
I am able to do things as well as most other people. (Disagree.)	47	10
At times I think I am no good at all. (Agree.)	48	33
I feel that I am a person of worth, at least on a plane equal with others. (Disagree.)	48	0
I take a positive attitude toward myself. (Disagree.)	49	10
I feel that I have a number of good qualities. (Disagree.)	50	7
On the whole, I am satisfied with myself. (Disagree.)	57	7
I certainly feel useless at times. (Agree.)	66	50
(N)	(44)	(30)

make the most difference was health. Among the 13 widows who said their health was fair or poor, all but one said they were often or sometimes lonely.

Patterns of Social Interaction

The way a widow is involved in her social world may also change over time. It is to be anticipated that soon after the death of her husband, a widow will do things differently than is the case several years later. In order to measure changes in social involvement over the period of adjustment in widowhood, the 1977 respondents were asked several questions on organizational membership, church membership, and visits and telephone calls of friends and relatives that had been asked in 1972. As shown in table 8-3, there was virtually no change in the degree of involvement for most of these types of interacting among the Sunshine widows.

Table 8-3 shows that the *level* of interaction with friends (whoever they were), organizations, churches, and kin remained stable; however, the identity of friends or the types of organizational affiliations may have changed. The largest percentage drop, in visits with relatives, may be interpreted to mean that kin withdraw some of their extraordinary support as widows adjust successfully to their new marital status. The slight decrease in frequency of church attendance is not statistically significant, but it is congruent with the widows' estimation of a somewhat lower priority of religion in their lives than had been the case earlier. In 1972, 52 percent of the widows told us that their religion had gained importance in their lives since the disaster; five years later only 37 percent made that statement. Fifty-three percent said that their religion had remained "the same" in importance since the disaster. Most of the widows did affirm in 1977 that religious faith had been a vitally important element in helping them to cope with bereavement: three

Table 8-3

Percentage of Widows Reporting Selected Types of Social Interaction, 1972 and 1977

Type of Interaction	1972 % (N)	1977 % (N)
Member of a least one voluntary organization	49 (43)	50 (30)
Officer in an organization	18 (38)	20 (30)
As involved in community life as I'd like	66 (44)	63 (30)
Church member	61 (44)	57 (30)
Attends church at least once a month	64 (44)	50 (30)
Visited relatives in past week	78 (44)	57 (30)
Visited friends in past week	75 (44)	67 (30)
Telephoned relatives in past week	75 (44)	70 (30)
Telephoned friends in past week	66 (44)	67 (30)
Wrote a personal letter in past week	55 (44)	43 (30)

out of four agreed that "My faith helped me more than anything else after my husband's death."

Summary

In general, the findings of the five-year follow-up of widows of the Sunshine Mine disaster indicate that morale, loneliness, and self-esteem all changed in a positive direction over time. The data also strongly support a "resources" approach to adjustment, in that the relatively well-to-do woman in terms of youth, income, health, employment, or marriage opportunities is the one who is happy and thinks well of herself. The 1977 findings corroborate the 1972 results showing that level of social interaction with friends or relatives has little bearing on morale, loneliness, or life quality.

Widowhood is perceived by these women as a time when independence is learned and when a confidant is appreciated. Dealing with children and coping with loneliness are seen as major problems. If a widow saw any advantages to her new unmarried status, such compensations usually related to being in charge of one's own life.

Popular culture includes the adage, "Time heals all wounds." Both the 1972 and 1977 surveys suggest that, in addition to time, the possession of material advantages—money, youth, health, education, employment—greatly facilitate the healing process. Advice to "become involved" appears helpful, especially when that means getting or keeping a job. Having friends and relatives, a new husband, or a religious faith to turn to also appear to be resources that widows used in achieving the positive adjustment they revealed in 1977.

Conclusions and Implications

This book has been an excursion into the lives of widows who became members of that "ex-role," as Lopata (1973) calls it, due to an industrial accident that killed their husbands. As we conclude, it should be emphasized that these widows acted independently in coping with their grief and recovered (or failed to recover) on the basis of their personal resources in the social contexts of their neighborhoods, family, and friends. Despite their large numerical presence in the Kellogg area, no "widow-to-widow" program was set up (see Silverman 1974). There was no widow on the board to administer the Educational Fund for the children who lost fathers in the mine fire. Seeking help via professional "listeners" was rare: only two of the thirty widows in the 1977 study sought the help of a social worker, public health nurse, or psychologist. A few had come into contact with such helpers, particularly during their relationship to public school personnel, and that interaction was usually oriented toward helping her children rather than herself. Professional helpers sought by the widows tended to be ministers, but the Sunshine women as a group were not deeply involved in organized church life and ministerial help seemed to be available only to the ones who asked for it. A similar lack of professional help to older Chicago-area widows is noted by Lopata (1979).

It appears to us that a predominant mode of adaptation to widowhood such as the continuity, replacement, or withdrawal-disaffiliation approaches discussed in chapter 4, had usually occurred by the time we first interviewed the widows six months after the fire. Moreover, the adaptation to widowhood, whatever the mode selected, was essentially the responsibility of the widow herself. For these women the quality of survivorship was largely up to the survivors, and those women who happened to have needed resources were advantaged over those who did not.

One way of dealing with survivorship is to read about it and analyze it intellectually. Many of the subjects cooperated with the researchers in hopes that their experiences could help others. Many were given preliminary reports about the progress of the study, and some wanted to preview what was being written. The senior author also responded to requests for reports on the research from interviewers, from two attorneys representing the widows and children in lawsuits, and from a social worker in Kellogg.

Having a confidant, a close friend, appears to have been a critical resource for many of the widows. As other research on friendship shows, people who have friends to lean on during personal crises weather the crises more successfully than friendless people (see Brown Parlee et al. 1979). We interpret the action of remarriage, present for half of the widows restudied in 1977, as a mechanism for dealing with loneliness (see Rubin 1979). Those widows who had remarried were lonely in about the same degree as adults generally, but those who had not remarried had high, atypical rates of loneliness.

In 1977 the Sunshine widows were basically well-adjusted women. Most said they felt good about themselves and about others. Although they were often worried about their children, there is no reason to suppose that those who had not remarried were any more concerned than are other single parents. One does have more responsibility when one must be both mother and father to one's children. For those Sunshine widows whose children are still at home and who have not remarried, the responsibility is great enough for them to say that dealing with children is their number one problem. It would be useful for future researchers to talk to children who survive a parent's death, thereby completing the picture of consequences of survivorship in a way not possible for spouses to do.

The widow's tendency to idealize the lost husband, explored earlier, is also a factor to remember. Lopata (1979) devotes a chapter to "Widowhood and Husbands in Memory," and the effects of such memories on child socialization as well as on adaptation to widowhood mode should be considered in future research.

It should be emphasized once more that there is great individual variation in how a widow uses the resources available to her. A psychologist who studied residents of the Coeur d'Alene River Valley following a disastrous flood found that some women in that area felt in control of their own lives; that is, they seemed to be internally directed (Thurber 1977). Others felt at the mercy of outside forces; their perceived locus of control was external to themselves. Presumably, had we measured such a dimension in our subjects, we would have found such differences among the widows. We do hypothesize that widows who were "internals," who felt they had control over their lives despite their bereavement, would utilize available resources more effectively than others.

The "externals," women who see the dominant forces affecting their lives as beyond their control, would be expected to be the widows most likely to hastily start new marriages, to impulsively sell their homes, or to move a long distance in an attempt to deal with their grief. We would expect many of them to adapt unsuccessfully, as one respondent said she had: "I jumped into another marriage too soon. It was a mistake, and I am now divorced."

In the context of survivorship, as in other complex social situations, we would suggest that a social exchange framework is a useful interpretive approach (see Scanzoni and Scanzoni 1976). Much as we work in the marketplace to exchange our time for money, which we then trade for clothing, shelter, or other things, exchange also occurs in the interpersonal realm. That is to say that individual and family decision making about dealing with survivorship occurs in a framework of a social exchange. One widow can decide to give up some of her independence in order to marry again and then her children can have a father, and she can play the role of wife and homemaker once more. Another widow may opt to retain her new independence, get her brother to help raise her children, take a lover, and seek close friends among her female coworkers. The exchanges, and the constraints and freedoms that accompany them, are consequences of opportunities, priorities, and available resources.

The adult developmental psychologists as well as the family development researchers also provide clues here (for example, see Kennedy 1978 and Goldberg and Deutsch 1977). As we age, we make choices. The life-choices, the ones that are more pleasant, are in interaction with the death-choices, the ones that tend to be less pleasant. However, over time even the life-death choices may come to reverse themselves. A person who is 90 years of age and who has had a successful life may view death as a pleasant alternative to life, whereas a widow who is 40 and who has children in high school may have quite different feelings about her own death or about life choices generally (see Glick, Weiss, and Parkes 1974).

Future researchers would be well advised to study life-change processes and to examine more specifically how widowhood, an event operationalized on a standard scale as the most stressful possible, is interpreted by the survivors themselves (Holmes and Rahe, 1967). We think that the interpretation of the widowhood experience in the light of the alternatives presented in the social world of the survivor would be most enlightening, particularly in cross-cultural or international context. Some headway into such research has been explored by Lopata, and we encourage more of that (see Lopata 1979: preface).

We also suggest the construction of social roles so as to give widowed persons a place. Uhlenberg (1979) concentrates his suggestions along this line to older women; we think Uhlenberg's ideas will work for women 40-60 years of age as well as those past 60.

We already know from a variety of international studies that widowhood is quite differently perceived, ranging from the Indian practice of *suttee*, in which the widow flings herself on her husband's funeral pyre, to the levirate custom, in which the widow is automatically married after widowhood to another member of her husband's clan, and to our own system wherein the survivor is viewed individualistically and is supposed to "get over it" and go ahead and achieve. These questions need to be answered. If the culture is less death-denying than our own, then is the role of widow planned and less stressfully adopted when enacted? If survivorship is a role thrust upon me, do I have a better chance to adjust if I have had some preparation for it?

We think preparation helps. We also think that "displaced-homemaker centers," proposed in Idaho and in operation in 28 states, can provide survivors, both women and their children and eventually men and their children, with some time in which to deal with their grief and a context in which to reassess and interpret their own lives and alternative life courses. Better outreach work by social service agencies and by churches would be an implicit and necessary part of such centers, as would be widow-to-widow programs.

Epilogue

It is now November of 1979. A visitor to Kellogg sees the Coeur d'Alene River twisting past the mine tailings and wandering back and forth down the autumn-touched valley, but the picturesque scene is deceptive. In January of 1974 that river flooded the valley and forced the evacuation of 800 families. No life was lost and there were few injuries, but the property damage was enormous. The 1974 flood was as bad as any the town had experienced. Local engineers now estimate the margins of the 100-year flood plain by reference to the crest of the 1974 waters.

By some standards the 1974 flood was a worse disaster than the 1972 fire. President Nixon declared the valley a federal disaster area in 1974. Requests for such federal action following the 1972 Sunshine Mine fire had been turned down. The bureaucratic message is not lost on area miners and their families: in the political scheme of things property-loss disasters are more important, or at least prompt more federal action, than do disasters where the major losses are husbands and fathers.

The 1974 flood had some positive side-effects. The river is cleaner than it has been for many years. Residues from the refining of heavy metals, which had gradually accumulated downstream, were washed away, leaving a cleaner river. The Federal Environmental Protection Agency also enforced air and water pollution standards by 1974, and together with the flood, has improved the fishing. The river is once again an attractive recreational resource, as it was at the turn of the century.

The "Silver Valley" is enjoying prosperity once more. The prices of silver and gold are at an all-time high, and there have been no recent labor strikes of long duration.

A mine disaster today would probably create both widows and widowers, for there are women apprentices in the trades, and even some of the miners are women. There is an adage about it being bad luck to have a woman underground, but the old prejudices have softened somewhat under pressure from federal regulations and affirmative action. There are also new and better enforced safety regulations in the mines, and the unions continue to demand, and get, safety drills of various kinds.

The legal disputes over whose negligence was ultimately responsible for the Sunshine Mine fatalities and who should pay compensation to the victims are still in process seven years later. Where cases have been pressed to judicial decisions, the courts have ruled against the widows and their children suing for compensation. However, out-of-court settlements by the mining firms have provided some recompense to victim's families. A recent article in the Boise newspaper summarized the litigation on behalf of victim's survivors as follows:

> Widows and children of the miners who died filed lawsuits against the state, and a miner's union, United Steelworkers of America. The lawsuit claimed both state mine officials and the union were negligent for not carrying out their duties to make safety inspections in the mine and demand correction of safety hazards.
>
> The Idaho Supreme Court agreed that the lawsuit against the state should be rejected, but said there was no reason why the legal action against the union couldn't continue in state courts.
>
> In 1976, a $660 million federal lawsuit was filed against various firms involved with the Sunshine Mine operation. After a long trial, a U.S. District Court Judge . . . ruled against the survivors.
>
> But 4 chemical companies settled with some of the lawsuits out of court for $6 million. . . .
>
> In a 4-1 decision . . . Idaho's Supreme Court ruled that the state could not be sued in the case . . . ; a District Judge . . . also granted summary judgment in favor of the Steelworkers Union. A state lawsuit over union activities is pre-empted in favor of federal laws. . . . (*Idaho Statesman*, Boise, September 14, 1979, p. 4B).

Despite the high volume of industrial activity, Kellogg's air is cleaner than it used to be. The smokestacks are higher, and consequently the concentrations of air-borne particulates in the immediate vicinity are lower than before. Some of the motivation for cleaning up the air came from a 1974 state study of lead poisoning among Kellogg children. It was found that children who lived under the Bunker Hill Smelter smokestack had higher levels of lead poisoning than did children in a comparison sample who lived in another county. As a result of that study, the mining companies shut down their company-owned housing near the mines, and families moved to safer neighborhoods.

Children who lost their fathers in the 1972 mine disaster are now seven years older than they were when we first interviewed their mothers. Some children who were born shortly after the fire are now in the second grade. Many of the older children whose fathers died in the fire have been helped by the fund established to help provide higher education for children of the victims. By 1978 there were 30 children assisted by these funds, and they attended trade schools as well as colleges and universities. Some children of men who died in the fire are themselves miners or are married to miners in the Kellogg area. Like local people generally they think there is little chance that such tragedy could happen again.

References

Brown Parlee, Mary, and the editors of *Psychology Today*. 1979. "The Friendship Bond." *Psychology Today*, October:43-66, 114.

Glick, Ira O., Weiss, Robert S., and Parkes, C. Murray. 1974. *The First Year of Bereavement*. New York: Wiley.

Goldberg, Stella R., and Deutsch, Francine. 1977. *Life-Span Individual and Family Development*. Monterey, Calif.: Brooks/Cole.

Holmes, T.H., and Rahe, R.H. 1967. "The Social Readjustment Rating Scale." *Journal of Psychosomatic Research* 11:213.

Idaho Statesman. Boise, September 14, 1979, p. 4B. Reprinted with permission.

Kennedy, Carroll E. 1978. *Human Development: The Adult Years and Aging*. New York: MacMillan.

Lopata, Helena Znaniecka. 1973. *Widowhood in an American City*. Cambridge, Mass.: Schenkman.

_____. 1979. *Women as Widows: Support Systems*. New York: Elsevier.

Rubin, Zick. 1979. "Seeking a Cure for Loneliness." *Psychology Today*, October:82-90.

Scanzoni, Letha, and Scanzoni, John. 1976. *Men, Women, and Change: A Sociology of Marriage and Family*. New York: McGraw-Hill.

Silverman, Phyllis R., ed. 1974. *Helping Each Other in Widowhood*. New York: Health Sciences.

Thurber, Steven D. 1977. "Natural Disaster and the Dimentionality of the I-E Scale." *Journal of Social Psychology* 103 (December):159-160.

Uhlenberg, Peter. 1979. "Older Women: The Growing Challenge to Design Constructive Roles." *The Gerontologist* 19 (no. 3):236-241.

Appendix:
Research Procedures
in 1972

On May 2, 1972, a fire in the Sunshine Mine of Kellogg, Idaho trapped 174 miners underground. Ninety-one men perished; 81 escaped the day the fire broke out and two more were rescued a week later. Six months after the fire we interviewed all the widows of victims of the fire who would consent to an interview, along with two comparison samples, one of wives of men who had been working in the Sunshine Mine at the time of the fire but survived and the other of wives of miners employed in other mines in the area.

Sampling

Lists of the widows and the survivors were obtained from the Sunshine Mining Company. All widows and survivors' wives were potential respondents; however, some could not be located because they had moved away from the area after the fire. Of the 77 widows, 11 had moved away; 41 (61 percent) of the 66 remaining completed interviews. Of the 72 married survivors, 10 had moved away; 81 percent of the 62 remaining completed interviews.

It was felt that widows who had migrated should be included, if possible; therefore, a questionnaire form of the schedule was mailed to 10 widows for whom forwarding addresses could be found. Three of the 10 responded; there was no attempt to follow up with additional reminders or mailings. These 3 are included in the widowed sample, bringing its total size to 44.

The comparison sample of other miners' wives was obtained via random sampling of miners' names found in the Kellogg-Wallace City Directory. The City Directory is always a year out of date, and so some of the names drawn from the directory-based sampling frame were people who had moved away. Contact with local telephone and electric companies as well as the local Steelworkers Union provided some up-to-date addresses. Additions to the sampling frame were made by obtaining lists of current workers in area mines; there were also randomly sampled. A total of 247 other miners' wives were approached; 52 percent of these completed interviews.

The Interview

The interview took about two and a half hours and was conducted in November 1972. It was generally conducted in the subject's home although

143

another site was available if subjects preferred, and two or three used the other site. Potential subjects were informed of the project by mail and then telephoned so that specific interview times and dates could be set up. Both in the letter and in personal contact, it was explained that researchers were associated with Boise State College with the support of a federal grant and were conducting the study to understand better the effects of the disaster and the nature of widowhood. Among the two comparison samples husbands were sometimes present during the interviews, although direct questions were asked only of the wives. Often both husbands and wives were intensely interested in the survey; many of the husbands had participated in the week-long search for the victims.

An interview is typically conducted by a trained interviewer who asks the respondent predetermined questions and records verbatim what the respondent answers. Interviewers, like the people they question, are subject to biases and prejudices, and the researcher tries to minimize interviewer bias where possible. In part, this is done by careful selection and training of potential interviewers, considered below.

Interviewer Selection and Training

Carol Harvey, the principal investigator, had attended high school in Kellogg, and many of her relatives and friends still lived there. She selected potential interviewers from her knowledge of the local social network. They were her friends, acquaintances, or friends of friends. She thus had the advantages of knowing the interviewers before the study and of having some knowledge about their integrity and willingness to respect the confidentiality of the subjects. Furthermore, because the interviewers were local women, they knew first-hand what it meant to live in a mining community. However, the use of local interviewers might have kept some potential subjects from allowing interviews. Having decided to use local interviewers, we had to accept this possibility.

Evelyn Montague, the field supervisor, was a former interviewer for the National Opinion Research Council in Chicago, and had master's degrees in both sociology and social work. She designed interviewer-training sessions which she and Harvey conducted. The interviewers were told of the Code of Ethics of the National Council on Social Work; the confidentiality of the subjects' responses was stressed, as was the basic right of the subject to discontinue the interview. (Note that no interviews were discontinued, even though many widows cried while being interviewed.) During the training session the interviewers practiced interviewing each other, familiarizing themselves with the interview schedule and learning to avoid "leading" the subject.

Contacting the Subjects

The principal investigator wrote a letter to each potential subject, explaining the nature of the study. The letter to the widows was slightly different from the one sent to survivors' and other miners' wives, but both forms stressed the need for cooperation. The letter also stressed confidentiality of responses and emphasized the subjects' right to refuse or to discontinue an unpleasant interview. After the letter of introduction was sent, the field supervisor tried to reach each subject by telephone or postcard, asking for cooperation and setting up an interview time and date. It proved to be impossible to reach every potential subject by telephone or postcard. A few widows without telephones were "tracked down" by tenacious interviewers, but for the most part those unavailable by telephone or mailing address were dropped from the study.

Refusals

Most of the widows had already made a firm decision about being interviewed as a result of the precontact letter, and they generally could not be persuaded to change their minds. Many had been interviewed by members of the press. It happened that while our interviewing was underway, staff people from a national magazine were also contacting the widows for interviews.

Survivors' wives and control-group wives surprised the field supervisor with comments such as, "I'm not involved; I didn't lose anybody." Would-be refusals among these women often agreed to cooperate when they learned that we wanted to measure community response and that people not widowed were also involved although in a different way from the widows.

Index

Index

About the Authors

Carol D.H. Harvey is professor of sociology at Boise State University. She received the B.S. degree from the University of Idaho, the M.S. degree in home economics from Washington State University, and the Ph.D. in sociology from Washington State University. Dr. Harvey has been engaged in widowhood research for twelve years, starting with her dissertation and continuing with the study of the widows of the Sunshine Mine disaster. She teaches classes in the sociology of the family, aging, and research methods.

Howard M. Bahr is professor of sociology and director of the Family and Demographic Research Institute at Brigham Young University. Professor Bahr previously taught at Washington State University, Brooklyn College of the City University of New York, and New York University. His interest in widowhood stems from a six-year program of research on homelessness and disaffiliation that he directed while he was a research associate at Columbia University's Bureau of Applied Social Research. His previous books include *Disaffiliated Man* (1970); *Skid Row: An Introduction to Disaffiliation* (1973); *Old Men Drunk and Sober* (1974); *Women Alone: The Disaffiliation of Urban Females* (1976); and *Ethnic Americans* (1979). He has also collaborated in a series of studies of relations between whites and Indians in the urban Northwest and is part of the team of the Middletown III project, a fifty-year follow-up of the study of *Middletown* by Robert S. and Helen M. Lynd. Professor Bahr teaches courses in research methods, ethnic relations, and urban sociology. He is presently working on a book about the strategies of family organization and stress management used by mothers of large families.